# SEX IN THE GOLDEN YEARS

# SEX IN THE GOLDEN YEARS

## WHAT'S AHEAD MAY BE WORTH AGING FOR

BY

## DEBORAH S. EDELMAN

DONALD I. FINE, INC.
NEW YORK

Library of Congress Cataloging-in-Publication Data

Edelman, Deborah S.
Sex in the golden years / by Deborah S. Edelman.
p.    cm.
ISBN 1-55611-207-6
1. Aged—Sexual behavior.   I. Title.
HQ30.E34      1990
306.7'084'6—dc20                                      89-46041
CIP

Manufactured in the United States of America

10   9   8   7   6   5   4   3   2   1

Designed by Irving Perkins Associates

*Dedicated to Irving and Rosalind,*
*married May 16, 1942*

The names of the individuals whose experiences are revealed in this book have been changed to protect their privacy.

# CONTENTS

## PART II
## SELF-PORTRAITS

## PART III
## THE PATH TO GOLDEN SEX

# ACKNOWLEDGMENTS

Writing this book gave me the chance to speak with older people about very personal things. I feel privileged that so many were willing to share their time and their stories with me.

In addition, I am fortunate to have had the help and encouragement of many friends and colleagues. My special thanks to:

| | |
|---|---|
| John Alexander | Ken Goldstein |
| Joseph Barbato | Alan Hall |
| David Bogle | Lisa Healy |
| Muriel Brown | Anita Isicson |
| Mary S. Calderone | Dorris Kingsbury |
| Fabio Coen | Adam Kuhn |
| Marcia Cohen | Jude Giabbai Mahoney |
| David Douglas | Angela Miller |
| Tom Dworetzky | Timothy Schaffner |
| Joyce Edelman | Susan Schwartz |
| Julia Edelman | Milton Sherman |
| Gerald Epstein | Jim Shortridge |
| Donald Fine | Larry Thompson |
| David Gibbons | Fredrica Wechsler |

# OPENING UP

As A child of the 60s, my generation is much less private about sex than the older persons from whom I sought information. Sex in the golden years has been a mystery, if not a surprise, not just because few have sought to study it. Today's golden agers grew up in a time when sex, at any age, was a secret. Husbands and wives hardly discussed it, let alone parents and children. The information that was available when couples married—the only publicly sanctioned circumstance for sexual activity—was limited and often inaccurate.

By the time I realized this, it was already too late; I had started asking questions, and older people were giving me their answers. Most were shocked, sometimes flattered, that I was interested. Maybe it was somewhat easier to talk to me because I wasn't a contemporary, I was innocent of the restrictions they had grown up with. Even the sexual revolution, which left out anyone over 30, had been waged before my time. Or maybe they opened up to me because they were simply tired of keeping it to themselves and not having anyone with whom to compare notes.

So what made me ask?

I was living in an apartment building which was

completed in 1929 and had many of the original tenants still residing there. As women tend to outlive men, most of these were widows. It was like living in a senior sorority house. Being surrounded by older women every day brought home the fact that I would someday be one of them. At first this was a frightening thought. I had the impression that I would always be young. I felt I bore no resemblance to the silver-haired ladies beside me in the elevator who reminisced about the days when the doormen wore white gloves.

Eventually, reality struck. Women who appeared younger than me were now joining us on the elevator. I realized that the older women had once been young, too. As I recognized the inevitability of aging, I wanted to learn whatever I could about it.

In 1984, I got my chance when I went back to school for my master's degree at the Columbia University Graduate School of Journalism. The title of my master's project: Women and the Challenge of Longevity.

The most remarkable thing that I discovered in my research, however, never made it into my master's project. In the course of interviewing women about aging and their health, several made references to their sexual activity. Sexual activity? It hadn't occurred to me to ask about that. I thought I was ahead of the game by reporting that people were living longer and that the medical profession was starting to address older patients' concerns, rather than dismissing them with a pat on the shoulder and a sympathetic look. Sexual activity was too big an issue to take on in my master's project. Instead, I devoted the next five years to it.

Originally, I was going to focus mainly on women, because older men have not been quite as neglected nor negatively protrayed. I decided that since it takes two to tango, however, I couldn't leave men out.

The first part of the book deals with facts and theories—what science and society have to say about aging and sex. The last section is full of suggestions of what people at any age can do to preserve or enhance their sexual health in the golden years.

The meat of the matter is the middle of the book, where older people have the chance to speak for themselves. As part of my research, I designed and distributed a questionnaire that could be answered anonymously, but I found that personal interviews—although they may be less "scientific"—provide a much fuller picture. I have included six full-length interviews, one with a couple, the rest with individual men and women. Each person's story is unique but contains elements which I found to be true for many others.

These "Self-Portraits" include details about their lives, their accomplishments, and their relationships, as well as about their sexual activity. After all, sexuality does not exist in a vacuum. For example, in Chapter Six, Bob White shares his fantasy of a house that is all on one level, with doorways and halls wide enough through which to ride a golf cart. That would make everyday life easier, at least for this man, and might result in more energy for sex, not to mention a clearer path to the bedroom. Perhaps home-builders and sex therapists should take note.

In fact, understanding the context of sexuality in later life appears far more instructive than the physiology. As gerontologist Ruth Weg says in Chapter Two, anyone can be sexually responsive given adequate stimulation but "genital response is only one measure of the total sexual experience." In other words, physiologically, aging need not hamper sexual activity. More sexually significant may be one's feelings about oneself and one's mate, one's expectations, general physical condition, alcohol or drug intake, mood, living situation, ability to communicate about sex, and whether one has a lover.

In the accumulation of details, a bigger, sometimes surprising picture emerges. For example, many women, such as Chapter Four's Helen Strauss and Rebecca MacDonald, report enjoying sex for the first time in the years after menopause. In most cases, this happened when they either lost or left their long-time mates and found new ones. The likelihood of this scenario appears greatest among women without daughters; Not having someone through whom they could live vicariously, they may have felt more compelled to seek first-hand experience.

Furthermore, I found much to suggest that today's golden agers were the fathers and mothers of the sexual revolution. It was fought by the young for the young, but it was the product of an older generation who, having grown up sexually restricted, encouraged their children to be sexually adventurous and to postpone or reject marriage.

Writing this book has been enlightening and inspiring. Youth may be filled with energy and a burst of new ideas, but the golden years provide the time to distill what has been fermenting throughout one's life.

That which appears to transcend all goals is to love and be loved. And, as the people whose stories you will read showed me, it is never too late to achieve or improve a loving connection with another person.

There may be far more that could be said on the subject of aging and sex. This book, for example, does not specifically address the experiences of homosexual or underprivileged individuals, not for lack of merit but of opportunity. In the future, I hope to broaden my research or to see others filling in where gaps remain.

Among those that I interviewed I encountered a wide range of experiences and offer perhaps only a glimpse into the realm of possibility. I leave it to you, the reader, to draw your own conclusions and explore the possibilities further. A recurrent message in this book is that you deserve greater attention and information but that you have the last word on what is true or appropriate for you.

If this book succeeds in encouraging even some of its readers in their pursuit of self-fulfillment, happiness, and love, I will feel greatly rewarded for my efforts.

> Love is the link
> that binds my years
> as memories fade
> and friends disappear
> and all that I lived for
> passes on without a trace of remorse.
> I know my fate
> and we are good company—
> I trust it like the sun

that rises and sets—
and each day
makes me more grateful
for my passion.

—D.S.E.

# Part I

# SOCIETY COMES OF AGE

# CHAPTER ONE

# THE CHANGING SOCIAL CONTEXT

*Forty is the old age of youth;*
*fifty is the youth of old age.*

—Victor Hugo (1802–1885)

## WHO WRITES THE RULES?

"I'm 62 and sex has never been better. The kids are gone, I don't have to worry about getting pregnant and we're retired so we can make love any time of day, even all day, anywhere we want. Every day is a celebration; we've made it this far and we're still alive. I wouldn't trade in this time of my life for anything."

This doesn't sound like the asexual stereotype women were supposed to age into. Nor does it sound like the life grandparents were supposed to lead. Is this an exception or are our suppositions wrong? On what have we based our perceptions of aging and sex?

Anthropologists have found that the continuation of

sexual activity into older age may be related to the degree of social equality in a given society. "Sexuality is very much tied to the rest of the culture," says anthropologist Jay Sokolovzki of the University of Maryland. Among the Asiatic Indians, for example, where women are repressed, sex represents male domination and women embrace menopause as an excuse not to engage in sex. On the other hand, he says, in socially equalitarian cultures, such as the South Pacific Islands, sex is openly discussed from childhood, it is engaged in for pleasure as well as procreation, and it continues for both men and women throughout life.

In our society, sexuality in older people has been the object of ridicule and pity. The underlying assumption is that continued desire is pathetic and inappropriate, since sexual function, we have assumed, is diminished and unsatisfactory. We underwent a sexual revolution beginning in the 1960s but it was fought by the young for the young. In advertising and other media, sex has been largely associated with youth, while the old have received little or unflattering attention.

Health problems of older individuals have often been dismissed as unavoidable by-products of aging, or treated with drugs which have unsexy side effects, such as disorientation or impotence—generally considered insignificant in older people by the medical profession. (More about this in Chapter Two.)

But our youth-oriented culture is coming of age, older people are more vocal and less accepting of inferior treatment, and modern medicine is responding with greater sensitivity and resources.

## STRENGTH IN NUMBERS

Numbers are playing a big part in the changing picture. According to the U.S. Census Bureau, there are approximately 35 million Americans between ages 40 and 55 and another 50 million age 55 or older. And the numbers are growing as baby-boomers join the ranks of the non-young. By the year 2010, more than one-fourth of the total U.S. population is expected to be at least 55 years old.

Formulating aging statistics has practically become a national pastime. The U.S. Census Bureau estimates that the 85-and-older bunch, the "oldest old," will swell from the current 3.1 million to 15.3 million by 2050, or about five percent of the total population. Those are impressive figures, but several academic specialists believe the census projections are far too low and badly underestimate a continuing decline in mortality rates in later life. Numbers game players may argue as to the precise figures but there's no question that we're a graying society.

The majority of those graying are women. Women not only continue to outlive men, but they are living longer than ever. Life expectancy for women was 48 in 1900. Now, according to the National Center for Health Statistics, women can expect to live an average of 78.2 years. For men it is 70.9 years. According to the National Institute on Aging, women in the 65-and-older age group are the fastest-growing segment of the United States population. By 2030, about 64 million —one person in every five—will be over 65. Two-thirds of these will be women.

## MONEY

The 55-plus population controls $130 billion in discretionary spending power, or half the annual U.S. disposable income. Today's aging woman, in particular, has more money and influence than her mother. Working is nothing new to women, but now they are politicians, doctors, lawyers, and corporate executives, and they have more control of their money.

According to a report of the Conference Board's Consumer Research Center, a private firm, the over-50 population accounts for 40 percent of total consumer demand. Among an array of impressive spending statistics, the report states that this age group purchases 80 percent of all luxury travel, owns 77 percent of all the financial assets in America, and owns 80 percent of all the money in U.S. savings-and-loan institutions. That's no small change.

## POWER

Numbers are also drawing the attention of the government. It turns out that the elderly and the near-elderly are the most likely age groups to vote. Data for the 1980 and 1982 elections demonstrate that about one-third of all voters are age 55 or older.

Aging-related organizations are growing and gaining a stronger influence on politics. The American Association of Retired Persons, founded in 1958, now has a membership of 27 million age 50 and over, and 3,400 local chapters. Its motto: "To serve, not be served." With a membership fee of five dollars, that's a powerful budget. As Ken Dychtwald points out in his book, *The Age Wave,* "if AARP were to become an independent nation, it would be the thirtieth-largest nation in the world, with a population only slightly smaller than that of Argentina."

The Gray Panthers (74,000 members) and the Older Woman's League (20,000 members) are newer and smaller organizations but they are often mentioned in the news, and bound to continue growing in size and force. Before the emergence of such groups, it might have been hard to picture older people demonstrating, petitioning, and winning their points. Now political experts count the elderly as a powerful, organized force.

Because women tend to outlive men, they feel the social, economic, and political ramifications of aging more acutely, and constitute the majority of those active in these organizations. And as anthropologist Margaret Mead observed: "There's no greater force than a post-menopausal woman with zest."

But 85-year-old Maggie Kuhn, who founded the Gray Panthers twenty years ago, stresses that her organization is involved in many issues that are not only aging-related. "We're the tribal elders and we're concerned with the tribe's survival. It's an anathema if old folks are simply associated with Medicare and pensions."

## PRESTIGE

Marketers are recognizing the proportion and buying power of older people, particularly older women, and are creating new slogans and new media to match. Perhaps it started with Clairol's hair-color advertising slogan that proclaimed "You're not getting older, you're getting better." Then came a prime-time TV program, "The Golden Girls," which portrays its senior citizen characters as sexually interested, if not always sexually involved. Ratings have been high since the show's inception in 1985, with a current estimated audience at 30 million. The products advertised during commercial breaks are sports cars, cameras, and health foods, not Geritol and laxatives. The show is funny, topical, well-written, well-acted, and appeals to viewers of all ages.

*Lear's*, a glossy magazine "For the Woman Who Wasn't Born Yesterday," began tapping the market in March 1988. Since then, *Mirabella, Moxie,* and *Longevity* have joined in the competition for the golden market. Even the *New York Times* created a special supplement called "The Best Years" by January of

1988, luring advertisers with boasts of a million-plus readers who are 55 and over.

Every women's and health magazine now devotes articles to aging. Unfortunately, many of these articles focus on fighting aging as though it were a disease rather than celebrating the triumphs of getting older. Still, the increased attention seems to be having a snowball effect. Here's a letter from the October 19, 1989, Ann Landers column:

> Dear Ann Landers:
>
> Last Sunday I attended an art exhibit in Michigan. I was wandering around among hundreds of people when a young woman touched my arm and said, "You are a beautiful lady." Ann, I was thunderstruck. I am 88 years old and never considered myself anything special to look at. But I'm healthy and happy and grateful to the good Lord for all his blessings. Maybe this is what comes through in my face.
>
> What a delight to be told I am beautiful by a stranger. Every day this week I have been cheered by that lovely compliment. It gave my heart a lift.
>
> Please print this. It might give others an idea.
>
> —Mrs. E.C.W. (Kalamazoo)

The increased visibility and appreciation of senior citizens, whether the result of marketing incentives or cultural maturity, is certainly long overdue.

## GOLDEN AGERS OF HOLLYWOOD

Although films have generally limited sex and romance to the young, there have been some exceptions in recent years. A 1975 made-for-TV movie, "Love Among the Ruins," starring Katharine Hepburn and Laurence Olivier, depicts the love affair of an elderly couple who re-discover each other after being apart for 50 years. In another film, *Best Friends,* newly married Goldie Hawn is surprised when her elderly mother speaks to her frankly about her continuing sex life with her father. "Mother, all you ever told me was that when it was right, it could be wonderful." Shaking her head and patting Goldie's knee, the mother replies: "Even when it's wrong it can be wonderful." Then there is the 1971 classic film *Harold and Maude,* in which Ruth Gordon plays a 79-year-old woman who initiates a young man into the joys of sex and romance.

The list of older-conscious films in the 1980s is somewhat longer. In *On Golden Pond,* Katharine Hepburn once again portrays an active, loving mate, this time with Henry Fonda. *When Harry Met Sally,* the story of a romance between two yuppies, is punctuated by brief interviews with couples who have been married for 50 or more years.

Judging from the course of our cultural history, as the baby-boomers hit their golden years, we may see an avalanche of such films and television shows. Even an episode of "Thirtysomething" highlighted the still-loving relationship of a senior couple, parents of one of the popular show's main characters.

## THE ART OF AGING

Photographers have often used older people as their subjects, but usually as studies of wrinkles or grandparents. There are some signs, however, that photographers are expanding their older-consciousness. "Yesterday's Children," a photographic essay by Patricia Worth Simmons, attempts to present "the experience of old age from the older person's viewpoint." She matches quotes from interviews with the photos, which mostly show individual older people engaged in various activities. Two photos are of couples, and one is captioned: "Seems to me that marriage—I guess it's like old wine—improves with age." In the spring of 1989, a chic Manhattan art gallery presented an exhibition of photos showing older couples in romantic poses, sometimes naked.

Of course, even nudity of non-old persons is gaining opposition these days, so it may be some time before the older body is celebrated as a sensual subject, or until it is displayed at all. In the spring of 1977, at the Paul Mellon Arts Center in Wallingford, Connecticut, there was a striking exhibition of 4 foot by 6 foot paintings showing naked older couples seated on sofas, staring blankly at the viewer. Although the artist

31

was well-known—Georgia O'Keefe—very little has been seen or heard about those works since then.

## RETIRING STEREOTYPES

The sexual revolution fought sexual stereotypes but society still defines and evaluates people according to their age. Until recently, those over 45, particularly women, have been considered over the hill. In judging one another, we tend to focus on appearances, with a youth-oriented ideal of beauty. Postmenopausal celebrities like Joan Collins and Jane Fonda have helped to increase the age limit of our beauty queens but we still lack sophistication as judges. Rather than redefining the stereotypes, we need to increase our appreciation of character, intelligence, expressiveness, knowledge, achievement, warmth, style, and social skills—personal traits that can be found at any age.

After learning of my book project, a friend told me this joke which suggests—if humor can gauge social change—that we are indeed retiring stereotypes: A young girl asked her 80-year-old grandmother at what point sexual desire died and was told, "You'll have to ask someone older than me."

## THE NEW AGE OF MEDICINE

Older Americans have finally been attracting the medical profession's attention, since their health problems are becoming more visible and it makes economic sense to keep them healthy. Again, this fact is most striking with respect to older women.

However, the number of women aging does not alone account for the increasing medical attention. A more potent factor, says Dr. Lila Wallis, a leader in the study of women's health, is the rising number of women in medicine and the growing demands of women in general for more attention and better health care.

Echoes Dr. William Ledger, chairman of New York Hospital's department of obstetrics and gynecology: "Women have not gotten their fair share of health care mainly because the male-dominated medical profession has not attached the same importance to their problems." But, he notes, "things are looking up."

The increasing number of women entering medical school suggests this trend will continue. According to the Association of American Medical Colleges, in 1969–70 there were 952 female freshman medical students or nine percent of the total first year class; in 1979–80, female medical students represented 27.9 percent of the entering class, or 4,748 women; and by 1989–90, 38.2 percent, or 6,404 freshman medical students, were women. As these women graduate and enter the medical profession, approximately one-third of American physicians will be female.

Another trend, though it may be too small and too early yet to make headlines, is of physicians, male and female, entering the profession later in life than before. In the years between 1980 and 1990, the average age of first-year medical school students hovered around 24, according to the American Association of Medical Colleges. But the raw numbers show that there are many more medical students over age 30 in 1990 than in 1980. For example, in the 38-and older category (the upper limit of AAMC's breakdown), there were 131 new medical students in 1990 compared with only 23 in 1980.

One doctor I know, a philosophy major in college, decided to go to medical school at age 30 after failing to convince her husband to do so. "If you think it's such a good idea, why don't you go?" he told her. She explained to me one day in her office: "I figured I'd be nearing menopause by the time I had my own practice. Then I realized 'What's wrong with that?'"

A booklet on menopause displayed in Dr. Wallis's Manhattan waiting room illustrates how attitudes have changed since it was published in 1964. In a chapter entitled "The Best Years Ahead," the author offers this advice: "Join one of the organizations in your town that devotes itself to an activity that interests you: a gardening club, a sewing club, a civic improvement organization . . ." Since that booklet was written, a new generation of women has grown up and is gaining the power, money, and prestige to warrant a new line of advice. And women physicians, in particular, are responding.

"We have a vested interest in keeping the millions of women who are aging in a healthy, productive, and happy state," says Dr. Wallis, a golden ager herself.

But more female doctors and patients are not the only reasons for improvements in older patients' health care. According to Dr. Diane Meier, a gerontologist at Mount Sinai Hospital in New York, there are two other historical and practical explanations; first modern medicine has had more success with acute problems—broken bones, infections, heart attacks—than with chronic or cumulative ills, such as hypertension, arthritis, and cancer. But second, more research and new technology are helping doctors tackle previously inexorable health conditions.

"Researchers and the medical profession in general prefer dealing with problems that appear suddenly and that can be fixed with a specific remedy, like a mechanic fixes a flat tire," says Dr. Meier. "If a woman has a problem with her uterus, you take it out. But when a problem develops over time, that's more difficult."

Take osteoporosis, a debilitating bone disease affecting one out of four postmenopausal women. Detecting it used to be difficult, if not impossible. Until recently, the only noninvasive method of viewing the bones was with x-rays. "X-rays don't show anything until you've lost thirty percent of your bone," explains Dr. Meier. "And by that time you know you have a problem—and it's serious."

In the mid-1960s, however, a procedure called dual photon absorptiometry was developed which now permits researchers to accurately measure bone density. The procedure, physicians say, is painless. It is relatively safe (the radiation involved is equivalent to that of watching two hours of T.V., says one medical technician); it takes less than 40 minutes; and it is relatively inexpensive. This new measuring equipment allows doctors to follow and compare patients over time and to predict, based on bone density, which women are at risk of osteoporosis. "We can now look at the bone density of a 30-year-old woman and estimate her chances of developing osteoporosis twenty or so years down the road," says Dr. Meier.

Dr. Wallis, who is a professor of medicine at New York Hospital-Cornell Medical Center, points out that women may also have the astronauts to thank for research into osteoporosis. "Without NASA discovering that astronauts can also develop osteoporosis [from long periods in space]," she notes, "it probably would not be getting so much attention."

The enormously high cost of health care for patients with the disease has lent urgency to research. According to the National Institute of Health, osteoporosis and its associated fractures cost $3.8 billion a year. When nursing costs are added, this figure rises to $6.1 billion. Put another way, one in twenty hospital beds for patients over age 65 are being occupied by patients with fractured hips.

Research on sex in the aged is the last frontier. Sex has not been viewed as a vital function in older people, but it has begun to arouse curiosity. And as medicine attends to the older population's needs with greater sensitivity and resources, the so-called biological facts of aging and sex are turning out to be as capricious as our social stereotypes.

# CHAPTER TWO

# THE BIOLOGICAL FACTS: MYTH VS. REALITY

*Men Oh Pause*

*to enter me*
*before I dry and atrophy*
*before I lose my lust for lust*
*before my hormones bite the dust.*

*I've heard tell, if you don't use it*
*that, in time, you're apt to lose it.*
*Some say estrogen renews it.*
*With K.Y. Jelly I'll infuse it.*

—RONNIE KLASKIN, AGE 55

## HEALTHY SKEPTICISM

ALTHOUGH I'VE spent a lot of time putting this chapter together, I would understand if you were tempted to skip it because, like me, you have become a skeptic about "biological facts." I think that's healthy. The bi-

39

ological facts, as scientists have established them, are not necessarily etched in stone. Every day, established wisdom is revised. Scientists make mistakes and can miss the forest for the trees. Headlines conflict and confuse. One day we read that oat bran lowers cholesterol, then new reports show that it doesn't. What's the story with cholesterol anyway? Is it worth lowering? Well, you see, there's good cholesterol and bad cholesterol. . . . But will tomorrow's news tell us that we've got the good and the bad mixed up?

Woody Allen deftly captures these sentiments in his film *Sleeper.* He's just been defrosted after 200 years on ice when one attending scientist says to another: "Did you know that in his day, back in the 1970s, people actually believed that tofu and bean sprouts were good for you and that hot-fudge sundaes and three-egg omelettes were unhealthy—the opposite of what we now know to be true!"

That scene has haunted me ever since. Could that explain why hot-fudge sundaes and three-egg omelettes are still popular, in spite of modern medicine's warnings? Are people hedging against the possibility that today's medical facts will be tomorrow's fiction? How should one digest medical information?

Before I give you my answers and the biological facts I promised, here's one last stroke to complete the picture: Remember when physicians told mothers not to breast-feed their newborns, that manufactured formula was better than breast milk? And mothers listened. "At the time my first child was born, I would have felt barbaric to breast-feed him and that I was depriving him of formula," a 68-year-old woman explained to me. The doctor's word was God's. But then it turned out that God's recipe for mother's milk includes a special brew of antibodies, released in the very first sip after birth, which boost a baby's immunity against disease. No man-made milk can come close. Medicine men can be wrong, and I've found that common sense is a good measure of whether to follow their advice.

As consumers of medical information, we've come a long way. We've learned that physicians and scientists are not God. Their word is their own and it deserves to be questioned, no matter how conscientious they were in their studies nor how prestigious their credentials are. An apropos cartoon in the *Wall Street Journal* on March 16, 1991, showed a 60-plus couple watching the news as the anchor announces: "The AMA has shifted its position. It now says everything you previously believed is *not* good for you *is* good for you."

## BELIEF CREATES REALITY

It might seem ironic, even foolhardy, that I am encouraging readers to be skeptical of medicine since writing about medicine is my business and I count on doctors speaking to me. But I think I'm covered. Here's why: one of the hottest fields of research is psychoneuroimmunology, which examines how perceptions—that is, how you think—influence your health. Numerous studies show, for example, that ingesting a simple sugar pill can remedy almost any ailment if you believe that the pill is really a full-fledged medication. That phenomenon is called the placebo effect. In other words, belief creates reality. Conversely, if you believe that something will make you ill, it may gain the power to do so. Therefore, I've got science behind me when I say that you have the last word on what is true for you.

The only immutable biological facts are that everyone gets older and everyone dies eventually. Beyond that, it largely depends on whom you speak to and what you choose to believe. If you want your golden years to be healthy and sexy, you hold the keys.

## WHAT PROBLEMS?

Although the limited number of studies on post-midlife sex have focused largely on sexual dysfunction, researchers are discovering that sexuality is not only alive and well in the golden years, but for many older people these are the sexiest years of life. Even among 80- to 102-year-olds, a study at San Francisco State University found 63 percent of men and 30 percent of women enjoying sex.

Illness can interfere with sex, but as studies of aging increase, researchers are discovering that many problems seen as inevitable by-products of aging are preventable or treatable.

Recent medical and media attention to the problems of aging, such as Alzheimer's disease and osteoporosis, may make the "biological facts" seem worse than they are. A U.S. Senate Special Committee on Aging report states that "one out of five elderly have at least a mild degree of disability." But that also means that 80 percent are not disabled.

The report, based on a 1982 National Center for Health Statistics survey, also says that, contrary to stereotype, most older persons view their health positively. Even if they have a chronic illness, two-thirds of the elderly describe their health as good or excellent compared to others their own age. That means even illness doesn't have to stand in the way of feeling healthy.

## SEX-KILLERS: PRESCRIPTION DRUGS

Sometimes it's not the health problem but the treatment that hampers sexuality in the golden years. Many drugs commonly prescribed to older persons, including antihypertensives and antidepressants, can decrease sex drive or cause sexual dysfunction. Often these drugs may be unnecessary. And often older patients don't realize that they are experiencing side effects and not simply old age. Sometimes there are alternative drugs or alternatives to drugs. It may be easier to pop a pill, but, in many cases, changing behavioral patterns such as poor diet, lack of exercise, and smoking, may be just as effective—if not more so —without the side effects of drugs.

It's important to be able to discuss your particular

situation with your doctor so that you know the potential benefits and consequences of any treatment and can make an informed choice. Unfortunately, for many older people, talking about sexual considerations with a physician is awkward, if not fruitless. Inability to discuss sex, for whatever reason, is perhaps one of the biggest problems of today's golden agers. Ironically, it has been documented that simply discussing sex can do more to alleviate sexual problems than considerably more ambitious psychotherapeutic, behavioral, and other educational methods.

## FACT-FINDING FOLLIES

Recent medical school graduates may be more receptive to patients' questions, but generally it takes determination to get satisfactory answers out of the old guard. Alice, 67, told me the following saga of her attempt to talk turkey with her husband's physician. She was feeling courageous when she finally questioned Dr. Smith about the medication he had prescribed four years earlier. Her 69-year-old husband, Bill, had moderately high blood pressure, and—without any discussion of his diet or lifestyle—Dr. Smith had put him on a drug which is commonly prescribed to prevent heart attack or stroke. Two pills a day from age 65 until death to lower blood pressure and maintain it at the reduced level. "Is it absolutely necessary?" Alice asked in the interest of their sex life, not to mention their savings account. "Do you want him to have a stroke?" the doctor replied. End of discussion.

## STATISTICS VS. SEX

Dr. Smith apparently felt he was doing his job, and no one in his profession would fault him. He made certain calculations that doctors are taught to make and arrived at what he considered to be the right answer. Based on statistics, he knew that a 65-year-old man with moderately high blood pressure has a 15 percent chance of having a stroke sometime in the next ten years of his estimated life span. Studies of the drug he prescribed suggest that it may reduce the risk of stroke by 20 percent (assuming that the patient ingests it as prescribed). Therefore, by directing Bill to take it, he was cutting his chances of having a stroke by three percent.

According to the medical literature, the common side effects of Bill's antihypertensive are impotence (reported by nearly 70 percent of users, but my hunch is that many among the remaining 30 percent either didn't notice or didn't tell) and liver damage (45 percent). These side effects have not been considered "significant" disadvantages relative to the drug's effectiveness in preventing stroke. Dr. Smith's decision to trade off Bill's liver and sexual function for the sake of reducing the risk of stroke is standard practice.

Could Dr. Smith have prescribed a different drug to do the job without the sexual side effects? Often there

45

are other drugs to choose from which can achieve similar results with different, if not fewer, side effects. However, antihypertensives generally work in one of two ways: either they reduce the flow of blood, which inhibits erection, or they block nerves, which can inhibit ejaculation.

If one drug is no worse than the next, the question again becomes "Is it absolutely necessary?" Bill plays tennis three times a week already, so more exercise probably wouldn't make a difference. But he runs around the court with at least 20 extra pounds. If he trimmed the fat from his diet and lost weight, could that lower his blood pressure, thereby decreasing his risk of stroke without drugs? Science says yes.

It's possible that Dr. Smith considered suggesting that Bill go on a diet but knew the probability was low that Bill would comply. Look around. How many people are still overweight or still smoking? No, it's not that they haven't heard the bad news. Even once the evidence is clear, it can still take time to break old habits. Drugs are the expedient choice.

If Bill isn't happy with Dr. Smith's answer, he can make his own calculations. Is he willing to give up sex for a three percent decrease in his risk of stroke? Is he willing to give up hot-fudge sundaes for sex? It's up to Bill to decide how important sex is to him. At least he should know that he has the last word and that it is a pill, not old age, that is causing his impotence.

Bill's case is one of millions, according to Peter Lamy, Ph.D., professor of geriatrics at the University of Maryland School of Pharmacy in Baltimore. As many as 70 percent of older Americans take antihypertensives, and more than 32 percent take antidepressants, almost all of which have adverse sexual side effects. (It is currently impossible to obtain precise figures of how many Americans take these drugs as that information is collected only by a private marketing research firm, IMS America, which provides its costly services exclusively to pharmaceutical companies.) Corticosteroids, taken for arthritis, may produce at least temporary impotence. Painkillers reduce sensitivity, hampering even the pleasures of touch as well as the possibility of erection. Cimetidine (Tagamet), used to treat duodenal ulcers and one of the biggest selling medications in the U.S., can cause impotence. The potential sexual side effects of many other prescription drugs are still unknown, particularly in women.

These drugs cost golden agers as much as $12 billion every year. (Again, the precise amount is not yet public information. However, Steve Schondelmeyer, Director of the Pharmaceutical Economics Research Center at Purdue University, was able to tell me that the total expenditure on prescription drugs in 1989 was $32–35 billion, and that the elderly consume 34 percent. That means the elderly spend $10–12 billion a year on prescription drugs.) Pharmaceutical drugs are big business, in general, and golden agers are their key consumers.

Although older patients may be grateful to have drugs to treat their ailments, it is worthwhile to note the incentive physicians have in writing prescriptions.

A U.S. Senate survey made public in December 1990 said drug companies were spending more than $165 million a year on gifts, trips, and payments for doctors in hopes of influencing their prescription decisions. Senator Edward M. Kennedy, chairman of the Labor and Human Resources Committee, which did the survey, said such financial incentives to doctors increased the cost of medicines and the risk of physicians' prescribing inappropriate drugs. These expenditures are separate from straightforward drug product advertising and promotional efforts, on which the pharmaceutical industry spent more than $5 billion in 1988 in the United States alone.

The total loss of sexual pleasure from taking drugs cannot be quantified. Then there's the humiliation, the frustration, and the resignation that may not be necessary. As older Americans make it known that they are not willing to give up sex, physicians and pharmaceutical manufacturers may become more sensitive in their distribution of drugs. There's also hope that more research will clarify the ties between sex and drugs and suggest alternatives to sacrificing sex. In the meantime, if your sexual health is suffering, check your medicine chest before you blame your age.

## OTHER DRUGS THAT CAN KILL SEX

### ALCOHOL

Believe it or not, alcohol is a drug, and not a very sexy one. Despite the romance associated with a bottle of champagne, the romance that follows its consumption may be a letdown. Alcohol can decrease inhibition, which might stand in the way of sexual opportunity, but it also diminishes physical capability and sensitivity. We have laws against drinking and driving; if you're worse behind the wheel, you're not going to be better in bed.

In *You Are What You Drink*, by Allan Luks and Joseph Barbato, the authors point out that few lovers at any age recognize alcohol's ability to create exactly the opposite effects of what the drinker wants. They list these facts:

- People often drink to lower their inhibitions and feel freer sexually. Yet alcohol decreases sexual arousal and performance.
- Many men drink to be "manly." Yet too much alcohol can lead to an excess of female hormones in a male drinker and result, for example, in the growth of breasts.
- Individuals hope drinking will make them more expressive and appealing to others. Yet alcohol causes many to lose emotional self-control and

49

become too loud or too quiet—and avoided by others.
ers.
· Many people drink to feel good. Yet studies link alcohol to depression in some persons.
· Then there is the greatest irony of all: Many of alcohol's desired effects—feeling good, attractive, and freer sexually—can result from *thinking* that you are drinking when, in fact, the punch is pure.

Alcohol's sex-killing effects become more pronounced with age as metabolism and tolerance decrease. That means as you age it takes less and less alcohol to produce the same effects. While I heard repeatedly from the people I interviewed that alcohol left them high and dry in the bedroom, often they didn't realize for some time, if at all, that booze was to blame. "I wasn't drinking any more than I always had," recalls Martin Shaw, age 70. He attributed his impotence to old age until an alcohol-free night showed him otherwise.

Alcohol's long-term effects are more subtle. In men, heavy drinking destroys testicular cells, leading to shrunken testes. It often affects hormone production, resulting in total sterility as well as impotence. Chronic heavy drinking can also produce liver and brain damage that leads to excess production of female hormones and a feminized body appearance.

In women, chronic heavy alcohol use can damage the ovaries, causing menstrual and ovulatory abnormalities and a decrease in estrogen production. This in turn may lead to early menopause. Premature atrophy of the breasts, uterus, and vaginal walls and less lubrication in the vagina are common effects of regular imbibing.

Besides what alcohol does to you—or doesn't let you do—sexually, it also speeds the deterioration of nonsexual organs, including your skin. Memory loss, depression, heart disease, liver disease, tooth and gum decay, gastrointestinal problems, decreased immunity, sleep disturbances, and accidents are just some of alcohol's potential by-products. Add to that its empty, high calories and you've got a most unsexy substance.

The current definition of heavy drinking also may come as a surprise to many. "Today" show host Jane Pauley almost fell off her chair when Keven Bellows, former executive director of the Alcoholism Council of Greater New York, defined heavy drinking as *one drink a day or more.* I was the head of public information for the Alcoholism Council so I can tell you that that pronouncement created more than a little stir. But the fact is that alcohol is a potent drug. And remember, women need less than men to get the same results and less is more as you age.

Until now, I have been talking about alcohol use, not alcoholism, which of course has even more dramatic, damaging effects. Perhaps because a characteristic of alcoholism is denial of the problem, by the alcoholic and his or her family, it is a far more pervasive problem than most of us realize. Recent studies have shown that up to one-third of all hospital admissions and outpatient problems are caused by alcoholism. Yet, the medical profession often misses the diagnosis or fails to prescribe appropriate treatment, according to Joseph D. Beasley, M.D., author of *Wrong Diagnosis, Wrong Treatment: The Plight of the Alcoholic in America.* Even once alcoholism is recognized, the alcoholic must be willing to seek and commit to treatment.

If your mate is an alcoholic, it's particularly likely that your sex life and relationship are suffering and getting worse over time. It's also much more likely that you'll lose your mate to the disease or some related problem far earlier than you would otherwise. Here again the problem is not age nor is it inevitable. Rebecca MacDonald, a 62-year-old legal secretary, discovered that "sex can be beautiful" only after her alcoholic husband died. She credits a new, sober lover, therapy, and Al-Anon. Unfortunately, she spent 34 years in an oppressive marriage, and for many others, alcoholism continues to put a damper on sex and life in general.

Even for those who have never been heavy drinkers, alcoholism in later life is a risk. Usually, according to Alice Petropolous, Program Director at Pace/Parkside Recovery Center in Manhattan, "late-onset" alcoholism occurs in response to a perceived crisis, namely widowhood, retirement (especially for men), menopause, or the "empty nest" syndrome, when the children move out. Such "reactive" or "situational" alcoholism can occur at any age but the later in life it starts, the faster it progresses. "An older person may become addicted at a low level of alcohol intake in just a few months," says Ms. Petropolous.

Unfortunately, she notes, families and physicians tend to have a cynical attitude toward alcohol abuse in older people, feeling that "at their age it doesn't matter," and the problem, if not ignored, is rarely treated. Few alcoholism treatment programs are tailored to the older population and often there is an age cutoff of 65 or younger. However, some nursing homes are establishing alcoholism education and treatment programs and senior citizen centers increasingly offer speakers on the subject.

The key to therapy, according to psychiatrist Sheldon Zinberg, who specializes in treating elderly alcoholics, is social contact and support through peer groups, especially for those who live alone. "Alcohol is a drug of loneliness," he says. "You can't treat older alcoholics ignoring the context of their isolation." Using alcohol to ease the pain or to fill the gap after a loss may be tempting but it is not a solution. (For healthier alternatives, see Chapter Nine.)

As much as ten percent of the population is addicted to alcohol and another ten percent don't drink at all. For the rest, I'm not saying that you shouldn't drink, especially if you enjoy it in moderation, but recognize that alcohol may be the culprit behind any sexual difficulties and that it can lead to other problems. The choice is yours. Maybe you could save the champagne for after sex. And if you are taking any medication, talk to your doctor before you drink at all.

## NICOTINE

Most of us know that nicotine is bad for you in many ways. Impaired sexual function is just one of them. But maybe that's the one effect that would get you to kick the addiction. Besides shortening your life span and the time in which to enjoy sex, it shortens your breath and makes heavy breathing harder. It also constricts your blood vessels, possibly causing impotence in the short run and likely causing atherosclerosis or peripheral vascular disease in long-term smokers. There is also evidence that toxic changes in the blood from nicotine may affect sex hormones.

## ✓ CAFFEINE

If you're a caffeine fan, you can claim that you're drinking it for your sexual prowess, thanks to a study that linked the two. University of Michigan researchers concluded that drinking coffee may somehow enhance the sex lives of older adults, based on a study of 744 men and women over age 60. Of the married women who drank coffee, 62 percent reported being sexually active, in contrast to 38 percent of their noncoffee-drinking counterparts. Of the men in the study, only 32 percent of the coffee drinkers reported potency problems, compared with 59 percent of those who didn't drink coffee.

But are these statistics a clear indication that coffee perks up your libido? Not quite. According to the Johns Hopkins *Health After 50* newsletter, while it is true that the caffeine in coffee belongs to the family of drugs known as methylxanthines—powerful stimulants that heighten sensory response in the central nervous system—the apparent connection between coffee and sex may be purely coincidental. People who enjoy good health in their later years may be naturally more inclined to be sexually active than those suffering from a chronic illness. Likewise, because of their good health, they are also less likely to be concerned about the detriments of caffeine or be told by their doctors to give it up.

So while sexual activity and coffee drinking may be "positively correlated," as statisticians say, there is no indication of a cause-and-effect relationship. Therefore, the study should neither discourage nor encourage you to drink coffee.

My tendency to value common sense over science makes it hard to believe that an addictive drug, which has been implicated in prostate and other cancers, can be an aphrodisiac. On the other hand, pleasure is a key ingredient in health and sexuality, so if you enjoy coffee, a cup or two a day probably can't hurt.

## DEPRESSED LIBIDOS

Depression can be as debilitating as a serious heart condition, according to a study by the Rand Corporation in Santa Monica, California. In fact, it can be more disabling than most chronic physical conditions in performing routine, daily activities such as walking, dressing, and visiting friends. Moreover, says a report on the study in the National Institute on Aging's Research Bulletin, depression in combination with a chronic medical condition greatly compounds the dysfunction that may be associated with the medical problem alone. For example, the study showed that "patients suffering from depression and coronary artery disease were twice as likely to have problems with social relationships as patients with only one of these conditions."

Clearly, depression is bad news and it is one of the most commonly treated ailments among older Americans. To top it off, treatment usually consists of drugs which may make patients less depressed but more socially dysfunctional (antidepressives can cause dizziness, forgetfulness, and lethargy, as well as sexual dysfunction).

But getting older may not be as depressing as it sounds. Depression may be a side effect of medication taken for some other ailment. And a study by Yale psychiatrist Myrna Weissman found no difference in depressive symptoms, their severity, or precipitating life stresses between three groups: patients younger than 45, those between ages 45 and 55, and those 56 and older. Furthermore, depression is one of the most responsive problems to nonpharmaceutical therapy, such as exercise, social contact, and sunlight.

## SO WHAT REALLY HAPPENS?

In the absence of disease or sex-killing drugs, here's what science says you can expect to happen sexually as you age:

### WOMEN

Descriptions in the medical literature of sexuality in older women usually focus on the potential discomfort and reduction of pleasurable sensation during intercourse due to thinner vaginal walls and decreased secretions. New data indicate, however, that while some women experience a decrease in sexual desire after menopause, others become more interested in sex and most are not affected one way or another.

Alfred Kinsey's maverick 1953 report *Sexual Behavior in the Human Female* got the ball rolling when he suggested that women remain at a sexual plateau for many years more than men. He found that women's interest in sex is consistent from the late teens into the fifties and sixties but their rate of sexual intercourse does decline in later life, probably for lack of available partners or because the partners stop initiating lovemaking.

It took pop, nonmedical researchers, like Shere Hite, to pick up the ball and run with it. *The Hite Report,* published in 1976, includes explicit quotes from 3,000 women, ages 14 to 78, who responded to her sexual survey. She dared to ask questions such as: "If you had to choose between intercourse and clitoral stimulation by your partner, which would you pick?" and "Do you ever fake orgasms?" Still, a chapter on older women spanned only 20 pages out of 600.

In 1984, Consumers Union, publishers of *Consumer Reports,* specifically surveyed more than 2,000 subscribers over age 50, by mail, to determine their sexual habits, attitudes, and practices. The CU researchers found a wealth of data putting old myths to rest. For example, contrary to what one would expect from reading the medical literature, only 35 percent of the female respondents said they had experienced vaginal dryness since menopause. And more than 80 percent of married women past age 70 reported being sexually active.

A dramatic illustration of how far we've come in retiring myths about women, aging, and sex is the news released in October 1990 that postmenopausal women can reproduce. Six of seven women aged 40 to 44 became pregnant via test-tube fertilization and four gave birth to healthy infants, including twins in one case. The experiment "shows how arbitrary age cutoffs can be in determining a woman's reproductive ability," notes Dr. Mark Sauer of the University of Southern California, who published the results in the *New England Journal of Medicine.* In a related editorial in the *Journal,* Dr. Marcia Angell writes, "The limits on the childbearing years are now anyone's guess." What other limits might be erroneously assumed?

Look and you shall find. Women remain a mystery

because they are often left out of research. Sometimes findings are reported as though they are based on both men and women, but closer inspection shows that women were well outnumbered. The explanation I have received from researchers is that men are easier to study. This is argued in simple heart studies where male and female physiology is equally visible, so when it comes to studying sexual anatomy the knowledge gap is predictably wider. (Efforts to correct this are under way at the National Institutes of Health. In September 1990, NIH established the Office of Research on Women's Health to assure "that research conducted and supported by NIH appropriately addresses issues regarding women's health and that there is appropriate participation of women in clinical research, especially in clinical trials.")

There is a plethora of information on menopause, but—despite some progress toward accuracy—it is still difficult to separate fact from fiction. Even physicians looking for updated wisdom on menopause may find their sources disappointing. *The Merck Manual,* a 2,578-page physicians' guide to diagnosis and therapy, notes that "symptoms can frequently be influenced by the insight and understanding of the physician in managing the patient. When psychic factors play a dominant role, psychotherapy and mild sedation are indicated. If depression is severe, antidepressants may help." Translated, this means: "It may be all in her head so be nice, and if that doesn't work, give her sedatives." Not very productive advice.

A more enlightened gynecologist describes menopause this way: "The main marker of menopause is when a woman misses her period. She's most likely between 48 and 51 years old and either she realizes that she's reached the climacteric phase of life or she comes to me for a pregnancy test. Most women are relieved to find out they're not pregnant and that they don't have to worry about that anymore." Dr. Veronica Ravnikar, director of Menopause Services at Massachusetts General Hospital, also says that her patients frequently express relief when they find out it is menopause, and not a health problem, that is responsible for whatever symptoms sent them to see her.

Basically, menopause is an actual biological event in a woman's life but it is not the end of her life. Besides the end of menstruation, women can count on these changes: estrogen production declines, ovulation stops, and pituitary hormones FSH (follicle stimulating hormone) and LH (luteinizing hormone) rise dramatically. Women may, or may not, experience hot flashes and mood swings, which are temporary, and dry skin, vaginal dryness, weight gain, varicose veins, and sleep disturbances. Bone loss occurs in all women after estrogen levels dip, but this is not problematic for 75 percent of women. According to the National Institutes of Health, about 80 percent of women experience mild or no menopausal symptoms; about 20 percent report symptoms severe enough for the woman to seek medical attention.

The climacteric span is generally ten years. While there's no definitive word on whether the age of menopause is influenced by such factors as marital status, number of children, and oral contraceptive use, slender and athletic women tend to experience it sooner than their obese and sedentary counterparts. Smoking also appears to accelerate the onset of menopause. Again, the bottom line is that everyone is different.

The current consensus is that aging does alter a woman's genitalia, and this can—though it usually does not—have an effect on sexual functioning. As her estrogen and progesterone levels decrease, a woman may experience changes in the size and shape of her genitalia. Beginning about eight years after menopause, a woman's vulva will become smaller. Her mons, labia majora, and labia minora will also lose fatty tissue, and will shrink and flatten. A woman's clitoris gets slightly smaller, too, although this is not thought to have any effect on sexual sensation. Her cervix, ovaries, and uterus will also shrink. During orgasm, the uterus may contract spasmodically rather than in the rhythmic pattern of her younger years, but most women cannot feel—or do not care about—the difference.

The most cited anatomical change in later years is in vaginal tissue. The vagina tends to get thinner, decrease in length, and lose elasticity. Fewer glands are available to lubricate the vagina, which can make penetration uncomfortable. All these changes are called the "senile vagina syndrome."

But the senile vagina syndrome, despite its fateful-sounding name, is not inevitable. The best rejuvenator of the vagina, sex researchers are finding, is continuous use—that is, orgasm and sexual intercourse as often as possible. According to sexologists Masters and Johnson, even women without partners can retain the vaginal moistness and resiliency of their youth by masturbating at least once a week. In addition, Kegel exercises (see Chapter Nine), performed regularly, can help keep the vagina well-toned and elastic.

According to gerontologist Ruth Weg of the University of Southern California, the phases of sexual response in women may change over time. The excitation phase is generally longer: it can take five minutes, rather than 15 to 40 seconds, for an older woman to achieve vaginal lubrication, and it takes longer for the clitoris to elevate in response to stimulation. The orgasmic phase is shorter, with the decrease usually beginning around age 50, "unless the woman has been extremely physically and sexually active," notes Dr. Weg. Uterine contractions drop from two or three per orgasm to one or two. And, as in men, the resolution phase (the period of time required for the body to return to its pre-aroused state) is shorter. Dr. Weg stresses that "if excitation is sufficient, women at any age can be sexually responsive." Furthermore, she points out, "the genital response is only one measure of the total sexual experience."

While there may be physiological changes with aging that adversely affect a woman's sexuality, there also may be beneficial developments. Some researchers believe that a woman cannot reach the true height of her sexuality until she has had children, when there is greater capacity for pelvic congestion, which means she has more blood vessels in her genital tract that fill with blood during intercourse and make orgasms more intense.

With or without children, hormonal changes may work in favor of increased sex drive after menopause. The libido-influencing hormone, androgen, is present throughout a woman's life, but its effects can be masked by estrogen and progesterone during her reproductive years. After menopause, however, androgen circulates in the body unopposed, and may result in a woman's sex drive rising with age.

## MEN

Studies suggest that age-related changes in sexual capacity and experience are much more profound for males (or are they just more obvious, or more interesting to male researchers?). They may require more time and stimulation than before to achieve an erection and an orgasm; intercourse alone may not be enough. When they do have an orgasm, they may not ejaculate. But it is the psychological impact, more than the changes themselves, that can diminish sexual pleasure.

It may be that, as men age, their sexual needs become more akin to what women's have been all along. One of the most striking studies in the past few years was conducted by a nonprofessional researcher, columnist Ann Landers. She asked her readers to respond to the question, "Would you be content to be held close and treated tenderly, and forget about 'the act'?" More than 90,000 women cast their ballots. Seventy-two percent said yes. Of those, 40 percent were under 40 years old. These results and others suggest that women at any age need more than intercourse for sexual satisfaction. By the same token, I would submit that older men can be satisfied with more plain tenderness and less sexual intercourse than earlier in their lives.

Although sexuality in older men has received more attention and is somewhat better understood than in older women, there is still considerable room for research.

Currently, the general consensus among sex researchers is that until somewhere in middle age, the mere glimpse of hips swaying halfway down the block might be enough to produce an erection. But as men get older, they slow down sexually and it takes more time and more stimulation than it did before to achieve the same results. And many men begin to worry, which only makes matters worse. According to most sex researchers, fear of impotence is the greatest cause of impotence. Some say one-quarter of men are impotent by the age of 65 and one-half by 75. But Masters and Johnson assert that all but the tiniest percentage of impotence cases are psychological in origin.

Early data from research on testosterone, the male hormone, suggests that there is a male climacteric. Although there is no clear-cut marker in men like the end of menstruation in women, between ages 40 and 55 men's testosterone levels may drop substantially or at least become less consistent. Recent studies are also showing that during this "male climacteric" men may have all the signs and symptoms of the menopausal woman. Whatever the explanation, the older man, who has grown up with an emphasis on performance despite the sexual revolution, may feel he is losing his manliness. Retirement can amplify his sense of dwindling power and potency. Just when he has more time to spend with his partner and relax, he may be feeling anxious and inadequate.

This can be very frightening. Furthermore, older men, as well as older women, have suffered from a lack of accurate information on aging and sexuality. Men are also less likely to reveal their inner feelings, particularly their sexual woes, to their male friends, so they have even less idea of what others are experiencing, and each may feel his problems are unique. In addition, according to Dr. David Marcotte at the Kinsey Institute, men rarely discuss their sexual questions with a doctor. Even if they did, general practitioners aren't trained to deal with them. And few men have a long-standing confidential relationship with a urologist the way women often do with their gynecologists.

In general, the only person who is in on what the older man may be experiencing is his wife. But a middle-aged man experiencing his first signs of reduced sexual prowess as his wife is supposedly reaching her

sexual peak may not feel comfortable sharing his feelings with her either. In her book *Passages,* Gail
Sheehy notes that middle age is the time that men are
most likely to seek a younger partner, to escape from
their wives and their feelings of inadequacy.

If men better understood what was happening to
them and felt less pressure to perform they might be
able to enjoy making love as more than a sexual act.
Slowing down sexually doesn't necessarily mean the
end of a healthy sex life. It all depends on the definition of healthy. If we define it as having the virility of a
17-year-old then there may not be much to look forward to. But in Chinese culture, for example, men are
taught to value slowness. And there are increasing in-
dications in our society that men learn to enjoy sex
more as they mature. In her report on male sexuality,
Shere Hite writes, "In this study, most older men said
that sex for its own sake was no longer very interesting, and that they now saw sex basically as an important accompaniment to a strong emotional attraction
or feelings for another person."

That sounds very much like what women supposedly feel throughout life. So it appears there may be a
kind of sexual rapprochement in the golden years.


## MATE-LOSS: THE SEX DIFFERENTIAL

As Nobel prize-winning physicist Roslyn Yalow first
pointed out to me, the biggest obstacle to sex in the
golden years is the shortage of men. Women tend to

age alone because they outlive men by six years or so. In addition, women usually marry men who are older, putting the ratio of widows to widowers at four-to-one.

But there's hope that science will learn how to help men stick around longer. At a National Institute on Aging conference on "Gender and Longevity" in February 1989, participants addressed the question of why women live longer than men and concluded that men tend to adopt certain high-risk behaviors and have a higher death rate from heart disease. According to epidemiologist Constance Nathanson of Johns Hopkins University, atherosclerotic heart disease accounts for as much as 40 percent of the sex differential.

Social and behavioral factors account for another one-third of the sex differential making up the gender gap. Causes of death in men include high rates of suicide, automobile and other accidents, cirrhosis of the liver, lung cancer, and emphysema—all of which result from behaviors that society encourages or finds more acceptable in men than in women. Such behaviors include using guns, drinking alcohol, smoking cigarettes, and working at hazardous jobs. While some trends are beginning to change (for example, men are smoking and drinking less), Dr. Paul Holinger, a psychiatric epidemiologist from Rush Medical College in Chicago, said that violent deaths (homicide, suicide, and automobile accidents) continue throughout life at higher rates for men than women.

Other factors possibly contributing to the gender

gap may be differences in genetics or immune function. While sex differences at the genetic level are beginning to be understood, the scientists say, further research is needed to show whether genetic differences have a direct effect on longevity or whether they have a secondary effect (the genes determine sex hormones which in turn affect longevity). Also, although there is a well-documented decline in immune function with advancing age, researchers need more information on how the immune system is affected by age, sex hormones, and the genes.

Participants at the conference concluded that research on gender differences is still in an early stage, and more information will be necessary to gain a clear understanding of the variables controlling longevity. Meanwhile, current data show the gender gap will continue to widen during the next four decades as our population ages.

On the softer side of science, there is some suggestion that men may simply give up on life sooner than women. As the number of physician visits and health book sales show, women tend to be more concerned about their health than men. It also appears that women adjust more easily to getting older. The women who responded to my questionnaire frequently described getting older in positive terms: "I feel that I keep getting better both mentally and physically," writes a 59-year-old full-time writer from California. "I am constantly surprised that I continue to feel young and enthusiastic about life." Men, on the other hand, were more likely to describe aging in negative terms, saying they felt "less powerful," "less productive," and that "life is less meaningful." Since immunity, as science is finding out, is influenced by how one feels psychologically, longevity may have something to do with one's will to live.

Traditionally, the emphasis throughout a man's life tends to be on breadwinning and physical prowess. Many—not all—men hit retirement with a thud, and find that after 60-something years of life, they've lost their identity, possibly their self-esteem. They may also miss the contact with co-workers and feel more familiar with the office than the home. After decades of looking forward to retirement, they may suddenly feel like a soldier without a battle. In the bedroom, going for quality over quantity may seem like having to learn a new language when you are feeling tongue-tied.

Women, particularly in the generation that are now golden agers, may be better equipped to move smoothly through the years for a variety of reasons. First, they are less likely to have defined themselves by work outside the home. Their network of friends is also less likely to be work-related to begin with and so may be more stable, especially since their friends are generally female and live longer. They have experienced the radical physical changes of pregnancy and childbirth so the aging process may seem mean but meek by comparison. They want their soldiers to come home and they still have their children and grandchildren to keep them employed as a mother, if only part-time. And their sexual performance anxiety was never as great or as obviously measured as men's. A slower-moving, more cuddling mate may be just what they've been waiting for.

If there is validity to the hypothesis that one reason men die sooner is because they feel they have less to live for, what might make them want to stick around? Feeling needed, learning to feel sexy even if they don't get erections as fast or as often as when they were younger, and having interests that go beyond retirement. It may take a few generations to find out if and how well this works, but it seems worth trying. (More about this in Chapter Nine.)

## THE OLDER YOU ARE, THE OLDER YOU'LL GET

While we're on the subject of life expectancy, and how many more years you and your mate have to enjoy sex, it's worth noting that the more years you live, the more you have left to go. That may sound like a clever paradox, but statisticians have begun to differentiate between "average life expectancy" and "remaining life expectancy," acknowledging that "average" isn't accurate for all people. To find the average, you add all the figures together and divide by two. That means that people who died at age 9 and those who died at age 90 are all entered into the same calculation. But if you are now 60, anyone who died at an earlier age gets eliminated from the calculation of your "remaining life expectancy." In other words, although the average life expectancy for a newborn is 75 years, if you have made it to age 60, your life expectancy rises to 84 years. Once you hit 70, statisticians say you'll probably make it to age 86. By 80, they give you another nine and a half years, by 90, another five, and so on. If you get to be 99 years old, chances are, they say, you'll live to 101.8. That's still just the average for your age, but it's more than 25 years above the average life expectancy you started out with.

## LOVE-MAKERS' HIGH

Sex researchers have found that the best way to prevent a loss of sexual capability with age is to continue to be sexually active. Sex therapist Ruth Westheimer advised participants at an American Association of Retired Persons' annual meeting to "use it or lose it."

It may turn out that sex is the best medicine for more than sexual health. According to Dr. Helen Singer Kaplan, director of the Human Sexuality Program at New York Hospital-Cornell Medical Center, erotic activity—especially orgasm—may stimulate the body's release of certain neuroproteins called endorphins ("the morphine within"), the same soothing, painkilling, mood-elevating hormones that are probably responsible for "runner's high." Having sex, says Kaplan, has an analgesic effect similar to that which one experiences after taking a mild narcotic. In fact, some physicians are prescribing sex for arthritis sufferers as a means of physically distracting them and relieving their pain.

## YOU ARE YOUR OWN AUTHORITY

According to the National Research Council's 1988 report on *The Aging Population in the Twenty-First Century*, the health status of the elderly "is better than generally assumed, varies remarkably among individuals, and is changing as successive [studies] progressively challenge the definition of old age." The report was compiled by a committee of health care policy experts to serve as a guide for developing health policy and producing information on aging. Despite its technical tone, its recommendations are clear and encouraging. For example: "Data collection should take into account the positive aspects of aging rather than purely functional decline, disease, and mortality." Imagine what we might learn!

So far, modern medicine's forte is caring for acute health problems and prescribing quick fixes. In recent years, prevention also has become a popular medical pursuit. But if it's quality of life you're after, it's up to you to take the initiative.

As other times of life, being older has its ups and downs. And the same circumstances or events may have different sexual effects depending on the individual. If men and women were less apprehensive about aging, they might be able to relax and enjoy it more.

72

After all, the golden years are the greatest and the last chance. If you want your golden years to be sexy, go for it. And if you want to compare notes with other seniors, read on.

# Part II

# SELF-PORTRAITS

# CHAPTER THREE

# TAPPING THE SOURCE

*Literature has neglected the old and their emotions. The novelists never told us that in love, as in other matters, the young are just beginners and that the art of loving matures with age and experience. Furthermore, while many of the young believe that the world can be made better by sudden changes in social order and by bloody and exhausting revolutions, most older people have learned that hatred and cruelty never produce anything but their own kind. The only hope of mankind is love in its various forms and manifestations—the source of them all being love of life, which, as we know, increases and ripens with the years.*

—Isaac Bashevis Singer
(1904–1991) *Old Love*

Since this is a book about sex in the golden years, and since information and experts in this area are still in short supply, I turned to older people themselves to find out what the story is.

Today's golden agers are not used to talking about their sex lives nor to anyone being interested in what they have to say. Anyone born before World War II grew up in a time when sex, at any age, was a secret and information was scarce. Although the sexual revolution of the late 1960s and 70s fought sexual stereotypes and restrictions, the revolutionaries were under 30 years old and left the older generation—their parents—out. Our culture has been increasingly more open about sex—books about sex abound and midday soap operas now show couples in bed together—but our "openness" has been youth-oriented.

Just because we don't see or hear about sex in the golden years doesn't mean that it doesn't exist, but it might have been easier said than done to get chickens to talk turkey.

After lifetimes of keeping it to themselves, most of the people I met in the course of my research were willing—sometimes eager—to open up for the sake of this book. Even among those who were reluctant, some later changed their minds.

Each person's story is different and I couldn't possibly fit them all into this book. Instead, I am presenting six full-length profiles based on personal interviews—one with a couple, three with women, and two with men—to give you an in-depth look at what each of these people had to say and how they said it. These self-portraits include details about their lives in general—their mates, their children, their interests, and their health—as the context of their sexual activity or inactivity.

These are real people, not statistics. Your situation

or experiences may be different, but you will no doubt find many common issues, thoughts, and feelings. This is simply—at long last—a chance to compare notes.

# CHAPTER FOUR

# LATE BLOOMERS
## HELEN STRAUSS AND
## REBECCA MACDONALD

*Grow old along with me!*
*The best is yet to be,*
*The last of life, for which*
*the first was made.*

—ROBERT BROWNING (1812–1889)
*Rabbi Ben Ezra*

HELEN STRAUSS is a classic case of someone for whom
the best years of life, sexually and otherwise, began
after menopause. When I first heard her story, which
was one of the inspirations for this book, it struck me
as unusual. However, numerous other older women
subsequently related similar experiences to me. These
late bloomers perhaps most clearly demonstrate the
importance of one's history and circumstances—the
context—in determining the nature of sexuality. They
also prove that it's never too late for romance and sex.

Helen, now 82, is a quietly charismatic woman who

SEX IN THE GOLDEN YEARS

dresses elegantly, often with a hat to match her outfit, and appears taller than her five feet two inches. She was a virgin when she got married in 1943 because "that's what people did." But after 25 years, she got divorced. "I didn't tell my husband that I was leaving him because I was sexually frustrated but that was the main reason," Helen recalls. "I admit that I wasn't the sexiest of wives. I didn't realize how sensuous I was until I had an affair at 58."

## INAUSPICIOUS BEGINNINGS

As with many people I spoke to, male and female, Helen's marriage was not sexually satisfying, even—or especially—when she and her husband were newly-weds. In Helen's case, one reason may have been the basis on which she chose her mate:

"I was over 30 when I married, 33, I think. That was old in those days. I wanted to get married already and to have children. My husband came from a nice family, our families got along well, and he was very good-looking. But I wasn't in love with him. I thought I might grow to love him and it was somewhat romantic for a while but my feelings for him were never that strong."

In addition, just before Helen's wedding, her physician pronounced that she would need to have her hymen, the membrane at the opening of the vagina, surgically perforated to make intercourse possible. This procedure, which today sounds barbaric, was at that time as common as hysterectomies have become. Perhaps tampons have served to diminish the hymen's presence before intercourse is first attempted, but Dr. Irving Saxe, a practicing gynecologist for more than 50 years, also suggests that "we may have been rather preoccupied with the premarital condition of the hymen and performed hymenectomies far more often than was necessary." So for Helen, like many other women of her generation, losing her virginity became more than a private matter between her and her husband.

"The doctor told me that I would have to go to the hospital and stay overnight, and I wanted to have it done before the wedding. When I told my father he said, 'No, you'll have to wait until after the wedding.' And then—Can you believe this?—he told my husband-to-be's father who made me go to *his* doctor, to make sure that what my doctor said was right. All this before the wedding, and they wouldn't let me have the procedure, so our honeymoon was not much of a honeymoon. We had a nice time and we sort of made love but with no conclusion. So it was several weeks after we were married when we finally had sex."

## THE DARK AGES

Helen still had romantic hopes but little information and no one to talk to about sex. "My mother never told me anything, and even my married sister wouldn't discuss it with me." Her near-sexual encounters before marriage gave her dubious insight. One man she worked with had said, "I want to have you before I marry you." When she refused he told her that she would "grow together." As it turned out, his prediction seemed to come true. Above all, even once Helen was engaging in sex with her husband, their lack of communication—pardon the pun—left her in the dark. Although they had no way of knowing it at the time, nearly every older woman I heard from shared Helen's early sexual predicament.

"Once we had sex it wasn't all that great. He was a very cold performer. He didn't do any of those niceties, like say certain things or kiss my neck, and I never taught him how to be a better lover. What did I know? Maybe other women knew how to teach their husbands but I didn't. So it was not very special but I did conceive two sons."

## SOCIAL, NOT SEXUAL, FULFILLMENT

Having children was the predominant role of women until recently and in that respect Helen was fulfilled: "I wanted children and I got two beautiful sons. And they kept me busy so I wasn't that concerned with sex and whether it was good or not. I loved my sons—and so did my husband."

On the surface, all looked well. Helen and her husband had a nice house, belonged to prestigious clubs, and were very sociable. Just as they never communicated about sex, Helen didn't say anything when she knew that her husband was having affairs. "I didn't blame him," she says. "He was very good-looking, he had a seat on the stock exchange and a nice office so he could attract other women." But she didn't like it, and rather than stick it out as other women chose to, she decided that she would divorce him once both her sons were in college.

"When I told him that I wanted a divorce my husband begged me to stay. He liked our life together, he liked our home and being a couple. He told me that I could have all the lovers I wanted if I would just stay married to him. But I didn't want that."

## POSTMENOPAUSAL AWAKENING

By that time, Helen had found her own lover and "discovered that sex could be wonderful." Her lover, Jay, was a friend's husband and she felt badly about that, but she didn't expect him to leave his wife. "I just wanted out of my own marriage." As other women have told me, rather than feeling badly after menopause and the children left home, Helen felt liberated.

"Until I was about 50 years old I never really thought that I was attractive. When I was younger, especially before I was married, I was very concerned about how I looked. After a while, I guess when I wasn't concerned at all, suddenly it seemed that men were finding me attractive. I remember I was stopped at a traffic light in the car once, it was summertime and all the windows were open and a man pulled up next to me and started talking to me and asked me if we could meet for lunch or something. I was really surprised that he was interested. My husband never seemed to notice me but other men started showing interest."

Having discovered that men found her attractive, after 25 years of monogamy, Helen decided to explore her sexuality with another man. Still, she chose someone she had known for years and with whom she already felt comfortable.

"Jay was a wonderful lover. I had no idea how pleasurable sex could be. And of course, by the time we got together, I couldn't get pregnant anymore so there were no interruptions or worries. It was just delightful." She had read a book by a woman who had dry vaginal walls and whose husband was very unhappy. "The book made it sound as though all women would have this problem, but it never happened to me, thank God."

Helen left her home in the suburbs and rented an apartment in Manhattan. Jay would visit her at lunchtime and occasionally in the evening. "That was enough," she says. "I was in love and I had my freedom." And she still had her children.

"They would visit me here and were always crazy about me. The oldest went to college nearby and he would come here to dinner with his friends. So leaving my husband didn't mean giving up my children. I could never have done that."

## SINGLE AGAIN AT 70

Her affair continued for 15 years until Jay and his wife decided to move to Florida. He offered to get a place there for Helen but she refused. She didn't want to give up her apartment in which she felt she had spent the best years of her life, her mother was in a nursing home nearby, and she was becoming disenchanted with their lovemaking.

Helen explained that Jay had started to be impotent and "he wanted me to do things I wouldn't do." When I asked her what she meant by that, with some embarrassment she told me that he wanted to have oral sex. "I guess I wasn't ready for that. Younger people seem to think that's okay but that's not something that women of my generation did—not nice women anyway."

So in her early seventies Helen was suddenly single again, but the story of her love life doesn't stop there. At first she was lonely since she hadn't developed any close friendships during her involvement with Jay. Eventually she discovered that there were some single men in her building and she invited them to accompany her to events at the museums where she was a member. She didn't become romantically involved with them but she enjoyed their company. "It was nice to be able to call and say 'Let's do this' or 'Let's do that,' and they would take me and bring me back and they never expected anything in return."

## OLD FRIEND, NEW ROMANCE

Then on a trip to the West Coast to visit her son, she ran into a man she had dated before she was married. She hadn't taken him seriously because he was several years younger, but now they were many years older, he had lost his wife, and he was still interested in Helen. They saw each other every day for a week and shortly after Helen returned to New York she received a dozen roses and a marriage proposal.

"Louis had been very sweet to me and we had a lot in common but I wasn't sure. It was too fast and we hadn't made love." A month or so later Helen went back to California to spend more time with him. Since she was staying with her son and Louis lived with his daughter and son-in-law, they arranged to go to a hotel for a night to be alone together. "We felt like teenagers and spent most of the night laughing."

In the end, though, Helen decided not to marry Louis. She was reluctant to move to California and leave her apartment and friends. More importantly, she was concerned with Louis's health. "He had already had bypass surgery and I didn't want to end up caring for a sick mate."

## WHY NOT, INDEED

Helen says she doesn't regret her decisions and feels that life, especially the latter part, has been good to her. She is beginning to feel lonely again because many of her friends have either moved or died, so she is thinking of moving to a senior citizens community because "they have lots of activities and people to do them with." When I asked whether she was interested in having a lover anymore she answered, "Why not?"

## REBECCA MACDONALD

Like Helen, Rebecca MacDonald discovered the pleasures of sex in her late fifties, but in her case, that followed her husband's death. In fact, despite a far more traumatic marriage than Helen's, Rebecca wouldn't have considered leaving her husband or having an affair.

Rebecca, 60, was in different circumstances than Helen going into her marriage. Her husband was divorced and she had sex with him before they were married. Orphaned at age 4, she had a financially difficult childhood growing up on a farm with her grandparents. Her husband represented an escape and she says she "worshipped the ground he walked on."

But because her husband had already been married, Rebecca's Southern Baptist grandmother told her that she was committing adultery. "Consequently, anytime that I had relations with my poor husband, my stomach would swell up and I would be in tears because I was going straight to hell."

## AFRAID TO LEAVE

That was on the good days. Her husband's heavy drinking escalated to alcoholism and her feelings for him became more fearful than romantic. He was extremely jealous, constantly accusing her of infidelity, while he himself was regularly unfaithful. He would go for a drive with friends and not return until days later. On many occasions he became violent, punching holes in doors, destroying furniture, and threatening Rebecca. "Mac was like a Dr. Jekyl-Mr. Hyde and I was scared to death of him. I think that's one of the reasons I stayed with him. I thought if I left, he'd probably run over me."

Just before he died, Rebecca's husband thanked her for putting up with him all those years and said how much he loved her. "Whenever I asked Mac if he loved me, he'd say 'I married you, didn't I?' In the end he told me he just wanted to keep me on my toes. Well, he sure didn't make me much of a ballet dancer."

To show his concern for her happiness, Rebecca's husband told her to find "someone to take you dancing" and recommended that she go out with his best friend, Ken. Rebecca thought he was joking. Ken had been one of his drinking buddies and she wasn't interested.

But after her husband died, Ken called to ask Rebecca for a date, and with the enthusiastic encouragement of her son, she accepted.

## RECOGNITION AND RECOVERY

"Ken took me out to dinner, to one of the nicest restaurants I'd ever been to, and treated me like I was some really wonderful person. And he told me then that he had been in love with me for a long time." He also told her that he had been in Alcoholics Anonymous and sober for 13 years, and suggested that she seek counseling, too. "I looked at him and said, 'I'm not kooky,' and he said, 'It doesn't mean that you're kooky, Becky, it means that you need help in working some things through.'"

To get her started, Ken took Rebecca to see his priest. "My husband wouldn't go to a family reunion with me because they didn't serve drinks. And here's Ken going with me to talk to a priest. I thought it was unreal that anyone would care that much for me." She spent the next two years going to Al-Anon (a self-help group for families of alcoholics) and five years seeing a therapist.

Counseling and Ken helped Rebecca feel better about herself. "I thought it was my fault because I wasn't as pretty as Mac's first wife and I wasn't as smart, and I wasn't, uhm, well, there were so many things that I wasn't. But then I found out that there were a lot of things that I was."

Rebecca continues: "Ken was the greatest thing that ever happened to me. With him I wasn't afraid. If I was late coming home, [unlike Mac] he never said, 'Who were you screwing?' He knew there was traffic, he knew you could get tied up, he trusted me, from here till kingdom come."

## OPENING UP

Still, Rebecca felt awkward when she first became physically involved with Ken. "I'm not a 20-year-old and I don't have the figure that I used to. I didn't want him to see me without my clothes on. I would put all the lights out and Ken would say, 'What is wrong with you?' When I said, 'Well, you know, I've got wrinkles,' he told me, 'Well, I have a potbelly. Neither one of us is the youngster we used to be but that doesn't matter.' He said that he still thought I was gorgeous, and that really made a difference."

Although Rebecca says she didn't feel the "skyrockets" she had felt during good moments with her husband, with Ken she felt comfortable. "I could talk to him about everything and anything, and I could question him about different things. Like I never knew anything about oral sex, and I always thought that was terrible. Then I got this book called *Good Girls Do It* or something like that. And I said, 'Would you believe this!' And Ken said, 'Oh, you poor little thing.' So we talked about it, but I guess, being from the era I'm from or being the person that I am, I just couldn't get into that. But Ken never ever insisted that I do this or do that. Whatever I wanted to do was fine with him."

Rebecca and Ken socialized together but they agreed not to get married and not to live together. Although her husband had advised her to find a new man, he also admonished her not to put another man's name on her house. But Rebecca regrets following that advice and for having taken it a step further. "I'd go to a motel with Ken and stay at his condo, but he couldn't spend the night in my house because it belonged to Mac. And now I really don't give a rat's behind."

## EVERY DAY A NEW BEGINNING

Four years into their relationship, just when it looked like they would be living happily, if separately, ever after, Ken died of a brain tumor. "I could have really lost it then," says Rebecca. "He meant so much to me and suddenly I was alone again. But one thing I learned through counseling is to rely on yourself first and that every day is a new beginning."

Indeed, Rebecca feels that she is in her prime right now, and although she still misses Ken, she is currently dating a man she met through a friend. On their first date they went to see a scary movie and Rebecca recalls that she didn't think he would want to see her again after she dug her fingernails into him and threw her popcorn. "But he said he had more fun watching me than the movie. He said, 'I'd like to cook dinner for you one day. What are you doing Sunday?' And I said, 'Well, my girlfriend is coming over, but you can come cook dinner for both of us.' And he did.

"Even after that, I never thought I'd see him again because he's eight years younger than me. But he said, 'If you didn't tell anybody, they'd never know because you don't look older.' He's balding and has a little gray, too."

Sexually speaking, Rebecca says, "It's fantastic." Harold is often out of town on business, but otherwise they usually make love once or twice a week, and he's "very kind and gentle."

## FREE TO BE SELFISH

Rebecca sometimes feels badly because she doesn't care for Harold as much as Ken. "I don't think I want to allow myself. And I think maybe I should tell him that I don't want to go with him anymore because I'm afraid I'm just using him. But he seems happy just to be with me. He'll come around and we'll go have dinner or I'll come home from work and he'll have dinner ready for me. And he doesn't seem to feel that he's being imposed upon. He says he's happy."

Rebecca is happy that Harold is not a drinker. "He might have a couple of beers now and then, but he never drinks like he wants to get drunk. That's one of

94

the reasons I stay with him. If he drank to get drunk, good-bye Harold."

Like Helen, Rebecca values her independence. "I think maybe I'm getting selfish. I don't know if I'd want to spend the rest of my life taking care of somebody else and doing what they want to do. I want to do what I want. I served my time. I don't want anyone asking any questions about why I want another pair of shoes when I've got a whole closetful. If I'm buying them and I'm paying for them, then it's none of your business."

## FREE TO BE REBECCA

Unlike Helen, Rebecca has a girlfriend with whom she feels she can discuss anything. "Marion and I tell each other when we're constipated. We don't have any secrets. You have to have somebody that you can be open with and not be afraid that they're going to go down the street and tell. When I tell Marion something, that's as far as it goes."

Contrary to what she expected, Rebecca says she doesn't feel old. "When I look in the mirror and I see the gray hair, that's the only time I realize how old I am. But I go to aerobics twice a week, I'm on the go all the time, and other than high blood pressure, I'm as healthy as a horse. I do anything I want to do. I take hormones because I had a hysterectomy, so I don't have that vaginal dryness problem or any of those things that they claim you get."

95

When I asked Rebecca what she would tell others about aging and sex, she said: "I hope people don't have the feeling that sex is bad, because it's something beautiful. I discovered that at age 57. And there is life after 60. It's what you make it. I used to think that I would be happy if so and so did this or that. But you can't do that. You have to make your way. And don't ever feel that you're not as good as anyone else."

# CHAPTER FIVE

# LOSS LEADS TO DISCOVERY

## MARTIN SHAW

*No wise man ever wished to be younger.*

—JONATHAN SWIFT (1667–1745)

MARTIN SHAW, 70, had been happily married for 40 years and expected the rest of his life to be spent with his wife. When his wife died of cancer, he was "completely disoriented" and "didn't think that there would ever be anyone else."

No one is ever really prepared for loss but women, because they are known to outlive men, are usually less surprised by it. When the wife is the first to go, the husband often follows soon after. Why is that? It could be that the man is usually older and has a shorter life expectancy, but no one knows for sure. Some say that men are less adaptable and have a harder time starting over late in the game. But losing one's mate doesn't have to mean despair. As with Re-

97

becca MacDonald, Martin Shaw's loss led to discovery, of himself and of his previously abandoned sexuality.

## SURPRISE! IT'S NOT OVER TILL IT'S OVER

Martin credits women's "aggressiveness" for his new lease on life and romance. He says he wasn't planning on dating and didn't expect to meet anyone new. But one day, six or seven months after his wife died, a woman he met through work asked him for a ride home. "She was very forward. She was in her early forties, and the fact that she found me attractive was exciting enough, but we ended up having sex. It was great!"

Besides being surprised that someone wanted to have sex with him, Martin was amazed that he could reciprocate. During the latter years of his marriage, "sex was minimal," and for the five years or so before his wife died, they "hardly ever had sex." "We both accepted that. We just thought our sex drives had lessened. It wasn't that we didn't love each other. I wasn't performing that well and she said okay. It wasn't a bone of contention, I don't think."

## RECOGNIZING PREMATURE RESIGNATION

Before that, Martin recalls, they had "a good sex life." "When it changed we just thought that it was something that happens at our age. We just settled into a life without it. We still cuddled, but I missed [sex] psychologically. I thought it was part of aging and I felt resigned to it. So I was rather surprised after her death to find that I could be stimulated. It was like being born again."

In retrospect, Martin realizes that he and his wife had called it quits on sex too soon. "Perhaps we could have benefited from sex therapy but it never occurred to us," he says. He was hardly encouraged when he sought advice from a urologist, whom he had gone to about a bladder infection. "I mentioned my low sex drive and performance capability, and he suggested that I take testosterone. But he wasn't terribly interested and there was no follow-up. He was embarrassed by the subject." Martin took testosterone for a while but he didn't see any difference.

## BOOZE BLUES

A more potent solution might have been to curtail his drinking, but Martin didn't recognize the possible connection with his decreased sexual prowess until just after his wife's death. "I was drinking a fair amount at that time. I was having a couple of stiff whiskeys every night. I told myself that it was only two drinks but I'd put half ice, half whiskey, and some water in a glass, so really I was drinking four to five shots per drink. I remember feeling very tired in the morning, so there's a good chance it was hampering my activity in the evening, too."

Martin says his wife never commented on his drinking and he never drank after dinner. "I wasn't drinking to the point of acting drunk, but I guess I was gradually drinking more. It was probably affecting me in many more ways, not just sexually, than when I was younger." Even if he wasn't drinking more, his body probably wasn't metabolizing the alcohol as fast as it used to.

Three or four months after his wife died, he quit drinking. "Now I have a martini every three months or so. Since then, I've noticed a big difference in my alertness and ability to work. And maybe that's why I'm able to be more sexually active."

## TUNING UP

Martin also started swimming after his wife died, which may help account for his improved sexual as well as general physical fitness. "I think that swimming has made a big difference. I didn't exercise much before age 60, but maybe the bladder problems started me thinking that I really ought to do something physical." In addition, says Martin, swimming gave him "something to do" after his wife died.

Now, he swims three times a week, 18 lengths in a 75-foot pool, after ten minutes of calisthenics to warm up. "I try to be careful. I know too many people who have bad backs. But if I miss one or two nights, I get very stiff." He says he feels a difference in his muscle tone and he doesn't have any more bladder problems.

Unfortunately, Martin couldn't share the benefits of exercising and teetotaling with his wife, since he only began after her death, but his positive action helped him move on with his life. And finding out that sex and romance could still be part of it was very encouraging.

## THE REMATING GAME

Martin continued to see the first woman he met about once a week for four months. Then he dated another woman, in her early sixties, for a while, but "when she wanted me to meet her family I wasn't ready for that, and we ended up breaking it off."

Some time later, he had a blind date with a psychologist. "She was in her mid-forties and very attractive. We went to bed together after dinner. I learned that women can be aggressive, and thank God! We were together about once a week for one to two months. At a certain point, though, I decided that we didn't have much in common."

Then he met a woman who worked for the government and was ten years younger. "We were together for three years but it ended unhappily. We lived together for two years but she was dissatisfied with me. She thought that I was unattentive. I didn't agree, but I couldn't remedy the situation. I was both sad and relieved when we broke up," he says. That was four or five years ago.

"Finally, I met the woman I'm seeing now, Marge. She's very nice and we've been together for three years. She's a widow, somewhat younger than I am, but everyone thinks she is much younger than she is. She's very attractive and with-it. We were planning to get married, but now we're not sure. So we're going on as we are. Usually we spend three nights a week together."

When I asked Martin if there were ever any overlaps between the women he dated he said no, but then recalled that before Marge, he occasionally saw an old friend from another city. "She had never been a lover before but now we were both widows. It was wonderful for three or four months—I would go there or she would fly here whenever we could—but we had our roots in different towns so it was difficult to work out a way of being together."

Other than that, Martin says he is a one-woman man. "I find it hard enough to handle one relationship at a time. It has to have meaning for me. I was faithful in marriage and we were married young. We're all tempted sometimes, but I was busy and I had other outlets."

Contrary to popular belief, Martin, like many older widowed men I spoke to, would like to be married again and finds that older women are the reluctant ones. "It's something that I'm used to. It's hard to break the mold and make yourself over at my age. I would like marriage—I feel it's more secure—but it is possible to be happy without marriage."

## NEW NEEDS, NEW APPROACHES

Although his feelings toward marriage and monogamy have been consistent, his sexual needs and responsiveness have changed. "When I was younger I had a tremendous sex drive and could come two or three times a night. Now, it's more of a psychological need than a physiological one. I need intellectual stimulation and a lot of physical encouragement."

What does physical encouragement mean? "I need a lot of handling. It takes a lot longer for me to become aroused and sometimes I can't orgasm. I just have to accept that. I miss the release but it's still nice. Of course, an orgasm is great, too. Especially at my age, I really appreciate it. The important thing is that we're two people holding each other who care for each other."

Martin didn't mention oral sex until I asked about it. He says he experienced it for the first time about "midway into my late sexual life" and that "it's great!" He and his wife had never had oral sex. "Maybe it was in the back of my mind but I never asked for it. My wife and I married as virgins. We didn't have oral sex either way, there were only so many things we did."

When I asked Martin if he feels any differently toward women than he used to, he said: "All men with any sensitivity feel differently about women than we

103

did forty years ago." His appreciation has increased further because of their sexual encouragement and understanding. He says he considers it a two-way street. "I always felt, sexually, that the greatest pleasure was giving pleasure because you get so much back. Unless your partner has pleasure, it's no fun—you might as well masturbate."

## MAKING THE MOST OF THE MOMENT

Couples who still have each other shouldn't wait for loss to make them improve or appreciate what they have, suggests Martin. He says he feels grateful that at least his chances for happiness and growth didn't die with his wife, and he looks forward to continuing discoveries, sexual and otherwise, with Marge. "We consider ourselves lucky to be healthy and to have this enjoyment. But we enjoy being together doing anything. Just holding each other as we fall asleep is bliss."

Martin says he doesn't have the energy "to push myself like I used to," but he's quite busy professionally. "Much of my motivation comes from wanting to keep my mind off other things." Several of his friends have died recently and he says he's been feeling particularly blue this past year. "First of all, losing a friend is sad, but secondly, it makes me realize that I'm nearing the end point myself."

Now, a very close friend of his has cancer. "What do you do? You work, you turn on music. A little sex is very, very vitalizing. It really makes you feel good that you can do it, that you *are* doing it."

Ironically, Martin says, he's been working too hard lately to see his girlfriend more than once a week. "I can't wait for more contact. It's like exercise, I guess, you have to do it regularly to stay in shape. And I find that sex is better when it's more frequent than once a week."

Although Martin once mourned the loss of his youthful potency and gave up on sex, as many older men do, he now feels like celebrating. "I might not be this fortunate at 80, but maybe then we'll just hold each other, and that will be nice, too. Life has its ups and downs all the time. I am grateful that I have someone special."

# CHAPTER SIX

# GIVING UP TOO SOON
## BOB AND SUE WHITE

*He who is of a calm and happy nature will hardly feel the pressure of age, but to him who is of an opposite disposition, youth and age are equally a burden.*

—PLATO (428–347 B.C.)
*The Republic*

HOW MANY older couples are not sexually active because they hit some snags, attributed them to aging, and then gave up on sex, and feel badly about it? Too many.

The following story illustrates the two most common causes of sexless sixties (or fifties or forties): performance anxiety and communication deficiency. Both have deep cultural roots and work together to strengthen the negative effects of the other. They also are problems that can be overcome.

Meet Bob and Sue White. He's 69, she's 67, and

107

they've been married for 46 years. Twelve years ago, Bob had open-heart surgery, and he and Sue stopped having sex. Okay, open-heart surgery sounds pretty dramatic. Maybe Bob is afraid sexual exertion will put him back in the hospital, or worse. But he's not afraid to play tennis nearly every day. Not just an hour of doubles but two hours, one on one. And when he injured his right shoulder so he couldn't use his arm anymore, did he stop playing tennis? No, he learned how to play tennis with his left arm. This is not a man who is afraid of exertion or who normally gives up easily.

## FEAR OF FACING DEFEAT

So what's the problem with sex? That's what his wife would like to know, but Bob refuses to discuss it. "I've tried to get him to talk to his doctor, but he won't," says Sue. In fact, she tried to get him to talk to *me* by inviting me to interview them for this book and neglecting to tell Bob precisely what I was there for. When I explained to Bob that my book was about sex and aging, not love and marriage, as Sue had told him, he exclaimed, "If it's about sex, I don't want anything to do with it," and began to leave the room.

Certainly the surprise confrontational situation his wife set up was not the most comfortable one for Bob; it was a desperate move on her part after 12 years of trying other ways to get him to open up. But Bob's emotional reaction to the subject of sex suggests that

108

it's not simply something he has decided he doesn't want anymore and feels good about.

Because Bob won't talk about sex—with his wife, with me, or with anyone else—we're forced to deduce what's going on from his behavior, what he does say, what his wife says, and other clues. Even without Bob's admissions—and his refusal to discuss sex is one of the most telling clues—we can make a strong case for what the problems are.

Bob's refusal to talk about sex is a common response to a "condition" he may be experiencing: performance anxiety. It's probable that Bob was not in top form after his surgery and any cardiovascular medication he was taking may have helped decrease his desire and ability to achieve an erection. Although temporary impotence can happen to men at any age, Bob, like many older men, may have interpreted it as permanent. Because of his embarrassment, rather than discuss the situation with his partner and make love without penetration until potency returned, Bob avoided physical intimacy altogether.

## UNHEALTHY ADJUSTMENTS?

Sue claims that she has adjusted and she has "gotten to the point where it doesn't bother me. . . You find something else to fill that gap." How so? Sue doesn't make any connection, and maybe there is none, but five years after Bob stopped having sex with Sue, she developed arthritic hips, diabetes, and hypertension.

"I got sick and so Bob showed his love by his care and he took very good care of me."

Sue explains that "because I couldn't run around and he felt guilty leaving me alone, we got to know a lot more about each other." For example: "With all of this hip surgery, I found out he knows all of the buttons to push: he can run a vacuum cleaner, he can do the dishwasher, he can do the washing machine, and he can do the dryer. It was interesting. All these years, he had been keeping it a secret." So Sue got the attention she craved but it seems a rather high price to have paid.

## DIFFERENT STROKES

Yet Sue and Bob say that they are very happy together. They have their differences, but they approach them with a sense of humor and mutual respect. Even aside from sex, their marriage hasn't been all smooth sailing, but they seem to have weathered it well. Here's a bit of our conversation so that you can see how they relate:

BOB: That's the only unfortunate thing about our life, and I say this in all sincerity. For some reason, I married someone who doesn't give a damn about golf, tennis, flying, skiing, or anything that's meaningful in life. And I don't give a damn about gardening and about arranging flowers or—

SUE: Cooking or going to the theatre.

BOB: There's not a thing, in terms of activities, that we are really compatible about.

SUE: He reneged. He made a bargain with me when we got married. He said, "Now look, we're going to be in the service, and you have to know how to do certain things in order to meet people, and one thing that I've been told is very beneficial is to learn how to play bridge." And so I said, "Okay, I'll learn how to play bridge, if you learn how to dance." Well, I've got master points in bridge and he still does a box waltz to the fox trot.

BOB: Well, that's because—

SUE: Yeah?

BOB: —of certain strange quirks in the left-hand part of my brain. That's not my fault.

SUE: It's pretty funny. A neighbor was saying, "You know, it's amazing to me that you and Bob have so much to talk about." She said so many of our friends don't. And we do.

Bob and Sue have a lot going for them. How might the sexual aspect of their relationship be improved? First, let's look at their history.

## MISINFORMATION LEGACY

From the beginning sex was a problem for them. Sue's parents told her not to do anything with a man that she wouldn't feel comfortable doing in front of her parents. Then when they first had sex, she says she "had a muscle instead of a membrane" and, like Helen Strauss, needed surgery before he could penetrate. Once they got over that hurdle, their sexual contact was limited by Bob's career. "My husband was in the Navy and we spent a lot of our first years of marriage separated because of the wars. So we didn't have too much time to fight," as Sue puts it.

When Sue sought information on sex she found that "those books were always put in a place where you had to ask for them and got a funny look." She laments: "It was twenty years before I found out that you could do more than just lie there."

Yet when it comes to talking to her own daughter about sex, Sue tells her that what really counts in a relationship is manners. "You may not have sex three times a day as you get older but you eat together regularly." Is that really what Sue thinks is the most important thing?

When it comes to eating, Sue and Bob realize now that there was room for improvement. "We went through a pound of bacon and a dozen eggs practically every morning," Sue recalls. "I thought I was feeding my family well when I was killing them." Bob believes he might have spared himself his arteriosclerosis: "I don't think you should be a complete idiot about diet or get into a hypertensive situation because you're worried about having eaten too much fat or red meat. But I probably wouldn't have needed the bypass surgery if my diet had been better."

## GIVE CHANGE A CHANCE

It may be too late to undo any damage diet may have caused, but both Bob and Sue say they feel better for having quit smoking and then drinking. For Bob, the incentive to avoid alcohol was tennis, which he started playing a few years after his surgery. "A friend of mine was constantly beating me. So I vowed that I would cut it out straight, not a beer, not a bit of wine, nothing. And after a few months, I started playing a little better, but it still took me a year before I got good."

Might alcohol have been hindering Bob's performance in bed as well as on the court? Unfortunately, like Martin Shaw, he had stopped making love before he stopped drinking. And Bob, unlike Martin, never gave himself a chance to find out what benefits sobriety might bring to sex.

## LOGISTICAL OBSTACLES

Sue and Bob also have some logistical obstacles to sex in their golden years. There's a joke that goes something like this: A priest, a minister, and a rabbi are discussing the origins of life. The priest says: "Life begins at the moment of conception." The minister argues that life begins at the moment of birth. Finally, the rabbi says: "You want to know when life begins?

When the dog dies and the children move out!" There may be a lot of truth to that. One of the most commonly cited factors contributing to greater sex in the golden years is the privacy afforded by the children leaving home. Conversely, if there are children still living in their parents' house, chances are their sex life is not what it might be. Although Bob and Sue might have other excuses, when they let their 40-year-old son move back into their house after his divorce, they were welcoming back the inhibitions and tensions of being parents plus the interruptions of having another person in their nest.

Another obstacle to their sexual freedom may be the design of their nest, coupled with their decreasing energy levels. "Bob was saying, it's too bad we didn't have San Francisco's earthquake here to knock down this house because we can't really handle the stairs anymore. This is [a split-level house] with four levels, and so he said it would have been very nice if someone had forced us to rebuild." What would Bob want instead? "I fantasize—maybe you will one day—of a house which is all on one level, without any sills or steps from one room to another. Each doorway is four or four-and-a-half-feet wide and you use electric k-cars like they use on golf courses to get around in." Although Sue complains that whatever energy Bob has he reserves for the tennis court, maybe with his dream house he would have some left over for boogie-ing into the bedroom.

These are all factors with the potential to influence sexuality but: the house could be changed; the son could be booted out; Sue and Bob have already improved their diets and cut out the culprits of nicotine and alcohol; and their sexual history, though it may explain a lot about their attitudes, is behind them. The main thing keeping Bob and Sue from sex in their golden years appears to be anxiety coupled with lack of communication.

## IT'S LOVE, NOT WAR

Here's a man who served his country in the Navy for more than 20 years, then became a pilot, an avid sailor, and an ace tennis player; he supported a wife and three children, and built a house with his own tennis court. He has been active in his community and says he pays "exactly what I owe to Uncle Sam, not a penny more or less."

The qualities that Bob values in himself and that account for his success in the Navy and in sports, unfortunately, aren't much help in bed. In her book *Lover to Lover: Secrets of Sex Therapy*, Nora Harlow's profile of "The Impotent Man" sounds like Bob and a lot of other men:

1. They are conscientiously responsible.
2. They are used to making decisions for other people—including their lovers. They make decisions fast. They stick to their decisions.

115

3. They have a record of competence at controlling their environment.
4. They do not expect—or, perhaps, even like—other people to help them, even their lovers.
5. They keep their lovemaking confined within a certain narrow range.
6. And, though they love women, they sometimes feel, for one reason or another, that they must maintain a distance from the female sex.

Although Bob may attribute any erection problems to his heart surgery or aging, it may have more to do with his being a "take charge, try harder, make things work" kind of guy. (By the way, this list of characteristics—at least 1 to 4—nearly mirrors the profile of a typical heart disease patient.) And instead of comparing himself with men his age, because there is very little information on sexuality in men past 40 and his peers are unlikely to discuss it, Bob's idea of what should be happening is based on the him of his youth.

Even if he hadn't already given up completely, he may have been waiting for a sign that his desire and erection capability had returned *before* initiating any lovemaking with his wife. But at his age that may be like putting the cart before the horse. As Martin Shaw discovered, unlike in his youth, it may require "a lot of handling" and "physical encouragement" from his mate to get his sexual juices flowing. Bob needs to decrease the pressure to perform while increasing his sexual contact and chances of responding. Yet, Bob prevents himself from discovering new approaches to making love and what he might be capable of when he cuts himself off physically from his wife.

## FEAR OF LOSS

Although Sue is relatively outspoken and independent, she may be somewhat inhibited in asserting herself in the relationship because of her fear of being alone. "We recently had a dinner party and I invited three women friends of ours who have lost their husbands. I've noticed that there are never too many single men at a party, but no matter what age, you don't want a single woman around, and that's unfortunate." Sue's identity, as she recognizes, is very much tied to Bob's and to being part of a couple. "Somebody asked me what we were going to do when we retired from the service, and that's exactly how I felt. That *we* were in the service and that *we* were retiring, just like *we* had babies. We did everything together." She admires her single daughter's willingness to venture out unescorted, but Sue can't imagine herself being "as adventuresome." "I would feel very uncomfortable going to the theatre or to a restaurant by myself. If I went, I would have to have another woman with me. I wouldn't go alone. And most of it is the company but part of it is the fear of being alone."

In some ways, though, as long as Sue and Bob have each other, their personal growth may be impeded. After several decades of marriage, if not sooner, patterns get set, roles get defined, and change becomes scary. It wasn't until Rebecca MacDonald and Martin Shaw lost their mates that they felt compelled to re-evaluate their lifestyle and self-image and make positive changes or improvements. After facing loss, they felt they had nothing to lose, and in their new relationships found themselves communicating more openly and being less inhibited sexually. For Bob and Sue, fear of upsetting or losing the apple cart may be keeping them from creating a better one.

## TAKING THE INITIATIVE

Still, Sue has begun to speak up for her romantic rights with positive results. "Last year, I told him that I just didn't think it was fair that he made dates with everybody but me and I wanted an afternoon of my own," she explains. Now, once a week, she and Bob go to lunch and then to the movies.

Sue says she appreciates that marriage takes communication and effort. "There was a study about boredom in marriage—well, marriage is only boring if you don't do anything to jazz it up. I try to let him know in a fun way that I feel neglected. The wife may not feel she's as attractive as her mate; I feel that Bob is more attractive. I don't want to feel sorry for myself and I let him know it.

"My mother, who was Irish, had a saying: 'A woman doesn't lose her husband. She gives him away.' I believe that. You have to let him know that you need him. And I do things to show that I care. Like I changed his cookies—I said, 'No more Oreos'—to keep him healthy."

Perhaps Sue needs to take it a step further. Martin Shaw credits women's initiative with his discovery that sex wasn't over for him. He would never have made an advance, thinking he was incapable of follow-through, but when it was the woman taking the lead, he followed. Maybe a woman feels less inhibited with a man she doesn't know well than with the one to whom she has been married for many years. And maybe the same is true for the man. But maybe Sue could break the sexual ice in her marriage by initiating playful lovemaking that doesn't focus on Bob's ability—or inability—to get an erection. (See Chapter Nine for more about this.)

## THE RIGHT TOUCH

Bob is a goal-oriented person, so cuddling and sexual stimulation that doesn't necessarily result in orgasm may seem unsatisfying to him at first. That's why Sue may have to take the lead.

> SUE: I'm not competitive by nature. I want to just have fun doing it, I don't have to win to enjoy it. He doesn't enjoy it unless he wins, if he doesn't win it's a horrible day.
>
> BOB: It's a horrible day if I play poorly, but if I played my best and I lost, that's great.
>
> SUE: That's why you always say your game was off.

Bob and Sue are talking here about tennis but their words may reflect their sexual differences as well. Traditionally and physiologically, women are more likely to experience intercourse without climaxing, and many women claim to enjoy it anyway. Confirming the findings of several other studies, responses to my questionnaire showed that most women, at any age, value the caressing and physical intimacy involved in sex more than intercourse itself. Most men, like Bob, at least for the early part of their sexual lives, measure their enjoyment by whether they came or not, whether they won or lost, not by how they played the game.

That doesn't mean that men can't learn to enjoy physical intimacy for the pleasure that it brings short of orgasm or even intercourse, but it may be up to the woman to teach her mate.

An incentive Sue can cite is the health benefits of touch. It's a proven fact that infants need to be held and cuddled in order to survive and thrive. Why wouldn't touch continue to be important to well-being throughout life? Many of the health benefits of sex are true of touch, such as increased levels of endorphin (the body's own painkiller). Maybe the aches and pains Bob complains of every morning, not to mention Sue's health problems, wouldn't be so bad if he and Sue stimulated the production of more endorphins.

The other rationale most sex therapists cite for focusing on the game of touch rather than the goal is that it can increase responsiveness. First of all, it heightens physical awareness. The shortest distance between two points is a straight line but, if you're not in a hurry, there may be many other more scenic routes between here and there waiting to be discovered. In addition, focusing on the scenery rather than the destination reduces the pressure and, by relieving anxiety, can increase the chances of blood flowing to the sexual organs.

## BEING ADVENTUROUS

What are the chances of Bob trying a new approach to lovemaking? Sue describes him as being "straitlaced" and Bob seems to pride himself on that. But he does have an adventurous side.

Here's an illustration: Bob wants to try drugs and plans to let himself when he hits 85, the end of his actuarial life span.

BOB: Marijuana, cocaine, everything that is now on the market. I'm going to try every one of them at age 85, and I'm going to consume them to the utmost and enjoy.

SUE: Of course, in his second breath, he'll tell me he swears he's getting Alzheimer's, so when he starts on this hashish stuff I say, "Yeah, at 85, you'll probably forget that you were going to do it."

BOB: Worse than that, someone said, "Yeah, at that age, you'll do it, and you won't get any kick out of it at all," and that's what scares me.

Maybe Bob is not totally straitlaced, he just needs to feel secure. He's waiting until the end to experiment with drugs so that he doesn't have to worry about their harmful effects (not to mention their illegality). Bob laments that "aging is not for sissies," and changes in sexuality may be among the scary parts for him. But with some reassurance perhaps he would be willing to experiment sexually before he's 85.

Martin Shaw lost his wife before he got to discover that he had given up on sex too soon. Bob and Sue still have each other and they are in love after 46 years. It might be tough to overcome one's fears and patterns, but as other people's stories show, it's not impossible and it's never too late. The potential benefits—greater closeness, pleasure, health—should certainly make it seem worthwhile.

# CHAPTER SEVEN

# THE JOYS OF INDEPENDENCE

## LEE ROBERTS

*We are always the same age inside.*
—GERTRUDE STEIN (1874–1946)

IN THE previous story, Sue White expresses a common sentiment when she says she pities single older women and dreads the day when she might find herself one of them. Perhaps the biggest fear of aging among young and old is of being alone. Baby-boomers popularized the single life for a while, but it seems that most people prefer to be mated. And although couples may split up at any age, being unmated in old age seems most prevalent and haunting. But as the following story helps illustrate, being alone doesn't necessarily mean being lonely.

Among the guests at a Christmas dinner I attended, which might have passed for a scene out of the TV show "Thirtysomething," was the hostess's 78-year-old aunt, Lee Roberts. Her niece had gone to visit her in Italy after college, and ended up living with her there for ten years. Despite the 40-year age difference, they were very close, and Lee easily mingled with her niece's friends.

Lee, herself, first went to Italy for a holiday after her divorce in her early fifties, and stayed for 25 years. She studied Italian, supported herself doing translation, typing, and occasional acting, and cultivated an international circle of friends. Having recently moved back to America, she continues to have an active, colorful life, and although she has had several lovers since her husband, she says "my greatest passion is for my freedom."

No, not everyone who is alone and older is unhappy about it. Quite the contrary, some people value their independence, especially after years of living with and accommodating the needs of other people. Being alone may have happened unexpectedly, as with Rebecca MacDonald and Martin Shaw, but it can prompt self-discovery and improvements that may not have occurred otherwise. Or it can be a conscious choice, made by someone who feels a greater need to pursue personal interests than to be accompanied.

For two reasons, this chapter focuses mainly on women: first, older women are more likely to be alone through greater longevity and having married older men, and second, independence is something today's older women generally experience for the first time in their latter years.

## OUTGROWING DEPENDENCE

While many of the female respondents to my questionnaire lamented the shortage of older men, others expressed their disillusionment with men as mates and mused or reported on the benefits of living without them. One 61-year-old woman whose husband died a couple of years ago says she's not looking for a replacement. "[Men] are overrated. They're often childish and certainly don't have all the answers I once thought." A 67-year-old retired nursery school teacher writes: "I was taught to consider men superior and their wishes to be more important than mine. Now I realize they are as vulnerable as women, perhaps more so."

Perhaps women are more likely to embrace independence because they have felt dependent on men throughout their lives and reach the point where they are tired of serving their husbands and children, and not themselves. In his book *The Pleasers,* psychologist Kevin Leman explains that men may get to retire from their role as provider but women find they are always expected to please. Some women demand retirement from this role, and by their golden years are either fed up or confident enough to make a break.

Society's sympathy for single older women may be misguided if not unwarranted. For example, one 60-year-old woman I met surprised me with her theory of why men leave their wives for younger women. Contrary to the impression that they are rejecting their aging wives, she argues that the older woman may have outgrown the needs or conceptions that drew her to the relationship and that she is the one seeking change. The woman may want to develop an identity beyond wife and mother and may reject her mate in the process. In turn, the man seeks confirmation that he's okay the way he is. Whereas the older woman now craves respect as an individual, younger women are receptive to the security that an older man appears to offer. Older women, says this educator and poet, "have a nightmare of their husbands becoming sick and needing care. Unless the man is younger, women get the burden of care. So when the husband leaves, it's liberation for the older woman."

This theory is certainly a departure from our usual thinking on the subject and so far the confirmation I have obtained is mostly in the form of nods. But there appears to be a lot of truth in it. Independence, older women may discover for the first time, whether resulting from death, desertion, or desired divorce, can feel more like a reward than a penance, contrary to expectations. Helen Strauss cited sexual dissatisfaction as the main reason she left her husband, and when she left she had a new lover in tow. But she discovered that she wasn't so much seeking a sexual replacement for her husband as a different lifestyle. She came to value her independence and ultimately turned down a marriage proposal in favor of her freedom.

## LATE LIFE IDENTITY CRISIS

Lee, like Helen Strauss, was unhappy in her marriage and decided to divorce her husband, although, unlike Helen, she did not have a new lover lined up and sexual dissatisfaction was only one of the reasons she wanted out. "I wasn't sure what was missing from my life but I wanted to go out in search of it," she recalls.

Lee's self-assuredness came in the years after her divorce; before then she was growing increasingly despondent until she reached the point where, she says, she "wasn't functioning" and went to see a psychologist. "First, the clinic gave me a Rorschach test and concluded that I was well-adjusted. I banged on the desk and said, 'I don't care what the test says, I need help.' " After one session, Lee says she screamed, "I've got to get a divorce."

But Lee's husband couldn't be entirely to blame for her personal crisis. Lee grew up as the eldest of six girls and, like most women of her generation, moved from her parents' house only when she got married, so she had never lived on her own nor developed her identity apart from her roles as daughter, sister, wife, and mother. "My parents used to travel a lot and so I was like the mother of the family. I would write to my mother and give an account of the entire family, but never about myself, it was as though I wasn't there."

This sublimated sense of self naturally influenced Lee's marriage and sexual relationship. "I wasn't in

127

love with him," Lee explains, "and I was learning to hate him more as the years went by because he was a misogynist. He was subtle. I'd get dressed up and he'd say 'That dress looks like an apron,' or like a bed-sheet. It was cruel, cruel, cruel. I would be yelling, but to myself I was scared to death of him. I used to dream of his dying, I thought every day, 'God, maybe he was in an accident.' Imagine living like that." As for sex: "I never enjoyed it, never. He had no idea—well, he was a virgin when we were married, we both were—and he used to tell me to read books. The whole thing was so revolting to me, I just couldn't take it." Not a very healthy situation, but Lee hung in there, like many women, for the sake of her son, who was 16 when she sought a divorce.

Going to a psychologist helped Lee realize how out of touch she was with her own needs and feelings. She describes one of their early sessions: "I said, 'Look, I'm not interested in sex, I really am not.' And he said, 'Stand up, look at what you're wearing.' I was wearing a tight sweater and a skirt. And he said, 'You're the sexiest thing around.' And I said, 'I don't feel it.' "

## DO UNTO THYSELF AS THOU WOULD DO UNTO OTHERS

Aside from Lee's overall dissatisfaction with her life, it was the illness and ultimate death of her sister, Ida, that pushed her over the edge. When Lee found out that Ida was ill, she insisted that her sister come to a hospital near her so that she could look after her. "Ida's husband was a gambler and she had been planning to divorce him before she got sick, so I knew he wasn't going to be there for her. And Ida's local hospital had refused to admit her because she was a terminal case. She worked for the Mexicans and Indians, she gave her time to raise money, yet they wouldn't take her," Lee recalls.

Lee visited her at the hospital every day for nearly six months. "It was almost like a painting; all the nuns and the sisters wore habits and looked like birds flying in the air. I would go down to the Mother Superior and ask for drugs since my sister was in terrible agony, and she would say, 'Don't tell me how to run this place.'"

Lee ultimately felt helpless in her efforts to comfort her sister. "Ida was a perfectionist when it came to eating and her cancer was in her intestines. She'd say to me, 'Please, get me some jam.' So I'd get her some and she'd say, 'Lee, you brought me garbage, when are you going to learn?' How did I know? Jam is jam and that's it."

To Lee, Ida's perfectionism and her devotion to a gambling husband seemed responsible, at least partially, for her illness. Lee, who was 42 when her sister died, decided that she had had enough of caring for others and wanted to start taking better care of herself.

## SELF-SUFFICIENCY

It took three years for Lee's divorce to come through—her husband didn't give up easily and waged a protracted legal battle. "His accountant doctored the books so they showed my husband had nothing. And in the end, that's what I got." But Lee felt liberated. "When I divorced him, I remembered the song 'Love and marriage, love and marriage, go together like a horse and carriage,' I'd sing it out loud. I was never so happy, even though I had twenty-five dollars in the bank."

Although Lee had taught dance off and on, she had done it more for fun than income, and had never had to support herself. "I didn't even know what the inside of an office looked like," says Lee. But she began teaching again to pay for business school, where she learned how to type. "I did a two-year course in three months. And a friend said to me, 'Lee, you don't have to be the best one,' and I said, 'No, but I have to be a good one.'" When she hit the job market she found that "wherever I went, because I wasn't afraid, they offered me work."

In fact, fearlessness came to characterize her career moves. "Once, at a magazine, I said, 'Please give me dictation, I need the experience,' and the editor said, 'I'd rather talk,' so we talked, and we talked, and I ended up writing copy for an ad. Later on, I had a beautiful office on Madison Avenue. But it didn't last

130

long. I was fired from every single job I had, I threw papers at presidents, I wasn't afraid of anybody. It never disturbed me because I always could get a job."

Finally, Lee decided that she had enough work experience and money saved to go to Europe. "I just had to leave America, for whatever reason," she says.

## SEXUAL LIBERATION

As anthropologist Jay Sokolovzki said in Chapter One, in egalitarian societies, women tend to enjoy sex much more and to continue being sexually active throughout life. Funny about that. Once Lee was divorced—or nearly divorced—she had her first lover other than her husband, and found it to be a different experience entirely. Before then, Lee says, "I felt that I was a completely frigid woman, that's why we had twin beds." But with Hank, who had been a student in one of her dance classes, "I felt wonderful, like I was sixteen." For starters, at 22, Hank was from a different generation than Lee and her husband, and was more sexually open. And Lee no longer felt she had to be "a good girl" nor "a good wife." She was free to enjoy sex, even to initiate it, and felt more relaxed and responsive knowing it was her choice, not her duty.

It had started innocently, Lee explains. She developed a group of friends at the school where she was teaching and Hank regularly attended their functions. "I felt that he was under my feet all the time." Then one day, he accompanied her home to change after class before going together into town on an errand. "While I was lying on my bed, I thought, 'What a pity I'm not attracted to him.' And then I saw him not as a young boy but as a man, and that's what started it."

What was Lee doing lying on her bed if she wasn't interested in seducing Hank? Well, remember, Lee was just starting to get in touch with her feelings and there may still have been some self-deception going on. The result here is what counts: Lee discovered, in her forties, that she was not frigid.

## FREEDOM TO LOVE—OR NOT

When she got to Europe, six years after her divorce came through and nine years after she first started therapy, Lee was much more in tune with herself, and after a few brief but sexually educational relationships, she fell in love.

"I never felt so good and so womanly as I did with Marco. Marco was perfect. And yet he was afraid. I had to teach him not to be afraid to love. That was a first." Perhaps Lee was particularly enjoying being the teacher this time, or maybe it made her feel most comfortable to be with someone for whom love was also a new experience. But ultimately, after several years with Marco, she decided to break it off. "Although he was emancipated in many ways, if we'd been married, it would have been different."

Lee was grateful for having found her way to discovering the joys of sex, but sex did not become the motivating factor in her life.

After Marco, she met an Englishman at a party. "It was mostly homosexuals there, so I just assumed that he was, too. He asked if he could take me home and I said fine. He wanted to stay, and I said, 'Don't be silly.' I wasn't the least bit attracted to him, though he was very nice looking, and I said, 'I thought you were homosexual.'

"Well, anyway, he stayed because I knew he was leaving the next day. And I was quite amazed. He was a very sensitive person.

"He had to leave early so I said, 'Well, I'm going to sleep on so you just leave whenever you have to,' and he left a note in the lock of my door, really teeny tiny, telling me what a wonderful night he had and that when he comes through again, he'll be in touch with me. And he did, and he left me the telephone number, but I never called it. I thought, 'What's the point of getting involved again, I have to straighten my life out more.' I didn't want to have to always think, 'someone's coming, I need to prepare myself.' I wasn't interested."

## THE SEARCH FOR SELF

It might appear, by turning down the Englishman, that Lee was afraid of involvement, but remember that when Lee left her husband it wasn't so much to seek another lover as to find herself. Even with Marco, whom she considered "the love of my life," she preferred to break up rather than to start playing to his expectations. Particularly, once she had experienced love and satisfying sex, rather than simply seeking more of the same, she wanted to find out what else there was to herself and to life.

Although Lee's direction may not sound too sexy, this is a perfectly healthy way to go, according to psychiatrist and author Gerald Epstein, who is affiliated with Mount Sinai Hospital in New York. The golden years, he says, can be the time when materialism and pleasure-seeking give way to spiritual pursuits. "Whereas the rationalist will see himself as what he does or what he has accomplished the spiritual person wants to know 'who am I?' and 'what's the purpose of being here?' " As one becomes more spiritually inclined, sexual energy is transmuted, and one learns that one doesn't need sex, or anything else, to be fulfilled. Sex may continue as an expression of love for another person, but the compulsion for pleasure or the release of tension evaporates as one becomes spiritually attuned.

Shortly after meeting the Englishman, Lee picked up a book by Krishnamurti, the late Indian philosopher, which marked a turning point for her. "For two years, I did nothing but read Krishnamurti. And even though I didn't go along with a lot of what he said, what I learned from him helped me enormously. To have your mind still, that's quite something. Not to look for distractions.

"I kept reading and re-reading, you have to live it to

absorb it, you see. And that's what I was doing. But I couldn't have read it if I hadn't reached the level I had. So I was ready. And then I realized that I didn't have to run out, that I didn't have to be occupied all the time."

Ultimately, Lee arrived at this conclusion: "The most important thing is to find out who you are and to learn to live with you. Plus, in the finding of yourself, a certain peace takes place in you because then you're not searching for something that you don't need. You see, the attitude that you have toward yourself you will have toward other people. If you can find a peace within yourself to understand yourself, then you can live happily with someone else."

## MARRIED BACHELORS AND OTHER ARRANGEMENTS

"It isn't that I'm disinterested in men," Lee explains. "If I found someone with whom I felt attracted, I'd be very happy. But he'd have to have his own apartment and think as I do."

Lee knows a couple who lives this way; they are married but the wife has her apartment and her husband has his. "And they both have their own work, he does translations and she does editing. She hates to cook, so she comes to him, like on a date, to dinner, even if it's every night or every other night. And they live very well together. So that's the kind of man that I would need."

This is not as crazy or unusual as one might think.

135

One 62-year-old woman I spoke with has been living separately from her husband for the past ten years, though they see each other regularly. "We were considering divorce, but by living separately we are able to have our own identities and still have each other," she explains. "He is the most important person in my life, we have our children and our history in common, after all. But we are not one person and you tend to forget that after thirty years in the same house."

## THE IMPORTANCE OF FRIENDS

With or without a lover, Lee has come to appreciate the importance of friends as a source of self-knowledge. She says she learns something new from each person she meets, and that she can feel like a different person depending on who she is with.

"Do you know that with some people I never open my mouth? Believe it or not. I have nothing to say because I get no feedback, I mean there's just nothing there for me. Whereas, I find that talking to someone like Pat, I can say to her what I couldn't or wouldn't want to say to a lot of people, and she does the same with me. Because we don't see each other socially. I know just a few of her friends, but when we're together it's only us, so I'm not involved in her life nor is she in mine."

One doesn't need to be living alone to achieve this variety of contact and feedback, but it seems there is a tendency to rely on one's mate as the primary reflection of who one is, when one person can only show us one side of who we are or who we can be.

## TODAY IS WHAT COUNTS

As you've heard others say elsewhere in the book, Lee was a product of her times in that she had little chance to compare notes or gain information about sex when she was young. "I got married knowing nothing about nothing. Do you know that for the longest time I thought babies came from the belly because my mother had an extended belly button, maybe because she had six children. Until 15 or 16, and nobody told me differently. You see, my sister, Jenny, she would tell us about menstruation, things like that. My mother was too shy, much too shy. As for childbirth, too, I was completely unprepared. My dear, I screamed and yelled, 'Why didn't *he* have this baby?' "

So she has come a long way, and Lee is grateful for where she is. "Telling you all this, it's like I'm talking about another person. I have been through a lot but I evidently needed all that suffering to become what I am today. If I hadn't learned anything from it, then it would have been a complete loss, but I grew from it. Even the husband that I had was my destiny. I had something to learn and, by golly, it was a hard thing.

"But I have had a very good life. I don't regret anything and I don't feel I'm missing anything. I just accept each day as it comes, and I'm happy to be here."

## THE ART OF LIVING

"The art of living," says Lee, "that's where my energies go, and that brings me life. It's a challenge to be happy. There's always a surprise, so I don't push anything, and I don't anticipate, I try not to be too compulsive. Today I planned to go to the library, and I thought, 'No, I'm not going to do it all at once, not in this weather, it's too damn cold.' And so I thought, 'If the occasion arises I'll go later.' That way you don't live with pressure.

"I find now that I have to rest more than I used to. I have a fluctuating pressure, and if I do too much, it goes up. So everything I do, even in the mornings, is like a dance. I do everything with a rhythm so that nothing is forced."

Lee's approach seems to work well for her; she looks healthy and her vitality could put a 30-year-old to shame:

LEE: In the last year or two, I have realized that I'm not as agile as I used to be—but I'm agile *enough*, I can still go down to the floor.

ME: And touch your toes?

LEE: Sure. I can walk with both my hands and feet on the floor. Can you?

138

## FEAR OF DEPENDENCE

Lee is motivated to keep herself in good health so that she doesn't have to depend on others. When she was in Italy, she met an 80-year-old woman who made a tremendous impression on her. "Cordelia was one of the most interesting women I've run into. She had been a very rich lady, but her children gambled away all her money. When I knew her, she lived in this little house in the hills. And she was always with her dog Buck, as in Pearl Buck, reading in the doorway. Her face was so lined but she had magnificent eyes. There were no toilets in her house, she had to pump her water from a well, she made her own oil, and someone would come to tell her the news because she didn't have a radio. But she had a bedspread that was so beautiful, it was made of linens that she had from way back.

"I remember her looking at the olive trees and saying, 'I think I should plant some more because that's a wonderful spot for them.' It didn't matter to her that it takes twenty years for an olive tree to grow.

"Cordelia was entertained by nature and didn't miss the money she'd lost. She ate when she was hungry and she slept when she was tired. And she was very happy.

"But half of her house belonged to the government and one day they took it back. She had to go to Florence to live with her daughter, and she died there.

"That's my only fear about getting old. I don't fear death, I don't fear being alone. I just need my independence."

Does independence preclude romance for Lee now? No, she says, in fact, "It's amazing, no matter how old you get you never give up."

## MOTHERS OF THE REVOLUTION?

Today's old were already married and ensconced in traditional roles when the sexual revolution occurred, but that doesn't necessarily mean that they had nothing to do with it. After all, children were fighting the institutions and mores that their parents had bought into, but where did the dissatisfaction that inspired the fight come from? It is arguable that mothers, in particular, encouraged their daughters to hang onto their independence as long as possible and derived vicarious enjoyment from their "liberation." Older women who did not have daughters, like Helen Strauss and Lee Roberts, may have been more likely to go for it on their own—once their children were grown, and they were in a position to move on.

On the other hand, just because older couples stay together doesn't mean they are not liberated or happy. The point of this chapter is simply to show that being alone in the golden years isn't necessarily accidental, pitiful, or unsexy.

CHAPTER EIGHT

# SEXUAL REVELATIONS
## GEORGE GIBBONS

*Age appears to be the best in four things—old wood best to burn, old wine to drink, old friends to trust, and old authors to read.*

—FRANCIS BACON (1561–1620)
*Apothegms*, No. 97

SOME OF the recurrent themes in the stories so far have been lack of sexual information, difficulties and dissatisfaction with sex in the early years, communication deficiency, and giving up on sex versus adjusting to changing needs. None of these hold true for George Gibbons, 62.

George was one of the most enlightening and enlightened individuals I encountered in the course of researching this book. Despite the supposed sexual repressiveness of the generation into which he was born, his attitudes toward sex and women are quite liberated, and have been since he was a young man. While his profession is unrelated, George says that he is "fascinated by women and by the differences between men and women." When he learned the nature of my book, he eagerly volunteered to contribute his observations regarding aging and sex, and summarized them this way: "I think the whole point of your book should be that you can have 18-year-old sex but as a 60-year-old, which is a fantastic combination. If a man can't get it up, it's in his head, and if he can't have multiple orgasms, it's in his head. And women at whatever age can be enormously desirable to me."

In some ways, George's story is similar to Martin Shaw's: he married, had three children and then lost his wife to cancer, and is now seriously involved with another woman close to his age. But George's early sexual history and experiences over time were quite distinct from Martin's.

## SEXUAL CULTURE GAP: SAME TIME, DIFFERENT PLACE

George's sexual history differs from the norm of his generation—for starters, neither he nor his wife were virgins when they got married—and he attributes much of this to the fact that he moved to Europe in his early twenties, the late 1950s, where sexual attitudes, he says, were more liberal.

"When you were a teenager in this country in the 50s, sex was a promise after you put the ring on, kiddo. It was not as it is today. When I went to Europe, the attitude was different and you didn't have to promise to marry a woman to go to bed with her. So one's sexual horizons broadened rather more quickly than they did living in this country. I don't know whether that would have affected a lot of guys my age who never lived abroad, but I would think it did."

> ME: So you and your wife were not virgins when you married?
>
> GEORGE: Christ, no. We didn't even think about it. And of course I was madly in love and sex was great.

## LOVING WOMEN FOR ALL THE RIGHT REASONS

Perhaps this early sexual freedom is responsible for George's attitude toward sex:

"I never slept with a woman just to sleep with her. There has to be an attraction and it has to be as much in the mind as in the body or I'm just not interested. I'm not interested in sex for sex's sake, never have been, even when I was a young guy. Looking back now, there were some women obviously very interested in me, but there was nothing there so I didn't pursue it, and I've always been that way. You know, if I can't make love to her mind, forget it. Now, I can articulate that, though I didn't think of it in those terms when I was younger."

## SELF-SUFFICIENCY BREEDS RESPECT

George considers himself totally self-sufficient—"I cook, sew, what the hell, I don't need anybody"—which he feels has made his relationships healthy. "I'm not in it for her ironing, I want her company. Some people say, 'Why give up your independence?' But I have my independence—I'm my own person and so is she—and together we have compassion. Sure it creates hassles, your money situation changes, but I want to be with a woman, it's as simple as that."

## SEX OVER TIME

When I asked George if there had been changes in his sexual relationship with his wife over time, he said, "No, until her operation, it was as good as it ever was." However, confirming the consensus, he noted that "[sex] starts to change when you have kids. There's just no way around it. Because of the physical demands of children—they're up at six o'clock in the morning, you know."

The absence of children, he says, is "one of the glories in my relationship with the woman in my life now. It's like being in love at 18, but you have the wisdom of years and you don't have kids to worry about."

Other advantages of latter life sex, according to George, as well as many others: "You don't have to worry about getting pregnant. And you can stay in bed all day if you want to and be as extemporaneous as you like, anytime. And believe me, that is a terrific thing."

## ILLNESS AND SEX

George was sexually active with and loyal to his wife until she had a mastectomy in 1970. "After her mastectomy, sex for her was just, just, she just was not—and it wasn't a conscious thing, she just didn't, she had no interest at all and I understood that."

ME: Was it a problem for you? Did you lose interest in having sex with her?
GEORGE: No, I didn't lose interest in having sex with her, but on the other hand I didn't—it was a strange thing. I didn't want to push her into it when she didn't want to. And I didn't want her to feel that because she wasn't interested it would hurt me.

Perhaps talking about it with his wife might have helped but this was not a situation George had experience dealing with. Instead, he turned to other women for comfort and sex. Meanwhile his wife relapsed in 1982 and then died three years later, after 26 years of marriage, when George was 56.

## AFFAIRS

"After [my wife's] mastectomy I had a couple of affairs, but I always made it clear when I was married that I would never leave my wife. I was very fond of them, but there was never any question that it would go any further."

Me: Were these long-term relationships?

George: One went on for years and years but I went months without seeing her. I'd call her up and say let's have dinner, and, you know. Easy relationships like that.

Me: Did your wife know?

George: No (emphatically). Would I ever tell her? NO. Never. That is one of the dumbest things, this American obsession with pop psychology, that you always must be open and honest. That's total bullshit in relationships. If you tell somebody, they never forget, right? They never ever are going to forget, period. That's it. And you can't go back from there. So these guys who confess, they're crazy. That's my view.

Me: Do you think your wife may ever have had an affair?

George: Possibly. But I never tried to find out. She was a very attractive woman and certainly there were opportunities. We lived on the coast and I worked in London so it was a fifty-mile commute. It's possible.

## SEXUAL ETIQUETTE: SAME PLACE, DIFFERENT TIME

Several years after George's wife became ill, George returned to America on business and was surprised by the results of the sexual revolution which had transpired in his absence:

"Good God, one had heard about singles bars in this country but what a revelation it was. It was interesting to suddenly be thrown into one-night-stands. I had several, a fair number, I suppose, but what I always did is call them the next day and see if they wanted to go out again. A lot of them didn't, which was fine, but I didn't go to bed with them, say goodbye the next morning, and never speak to them again.

"I've always felt, with rare exceptions, that women in their freedom might fancy a guy and go to bed with him the first time they meet, but that they are not totally happy with that. So I would always call them and I was friendly and if they wanted to go out again, we did. A couple I saw several times and others I didn't at all."

## IN PRAISE OF POSTMENOPAUSAL WOMEN

George says he has had many opportunities to go to bed with younger women, some of which he pursued, but ultimately he concluded that he prefers women his age.

"If you ask most guys, 'Gee, how would you like to have a woman twenty years younger than you madly in love with you?' they'd say 'Fantastic!' And if you want a male ego trip, it is. But I never looked on it that way. They were just women I liked and was interested in.

"I faced the fact that in certain ways you're a father figure. The same way that I think of women who are with guys who are much younger. She's a substitute mother they can go to bed with. To deny that is ridiculous. It might be great for an affair or a brief encounter, no problem, but not for the long term.

"I found that age makes absolutely no difference in a woman's sexual response, and the older they get, I think it gives them enormous energy to think they're still desirable, that a man still wants to go to bed with them, and not just for a quickie, but that they really want to have a relationship.

"The biggest thing is that they can feel less inhibited because they've lost the ability to get pregnant. Although I think a woman's behavior is often governed by a man's behavior, whether they feel that they can be as honest as they want to be. I think that's true of women at all ages. They're frightened to be too—I hate the word 'aggressive'—but too spontaneous. A lot of guys misread that."

## GETTING TOGETHER

Although George is a fan of women over 50, he has found it difficult to meet them. This seems ironic, since the biggest problem for older women, as my findings along with George's suggest, is meeting someone. "But they don't go out as much, and they don't go to bars. Occasionally, I'll see an ISO [in search of] ad in the *Washingtonian* from a woman in her fifties, but generally speaking, it's much easier for me to meet women in their thirties," says George.

## DRINKING AND SEX DON'T MIX

George recognized early on that drinking and sex don't mix:

"People are crazy if they combine alcohol and sex, especially when you are first becoming comfortable with someone, and you are exquisitely sensitive to their response, or you should be. You don't want alcohol messing that up. If I know I'm going to be with someone, I just don't drink, it's as simple as that.

"If you haven't been drinking, it's two thousand times better, in my experience, and I guess that's true for a woman, that response is dulled by alcohol. There's no question about it. Your emotional and psychological drives might be heightened in the sense that you become less inhibited, especially if you're a

149

woman, but on the other hand the physiological response is not the same.

"I've been with women who've been drinking a lot and Jesus Christ, they want to have sex, but orgasm, forget it. You can beaver away for hours and nothing happens or you get this little tiny response, I mean it's a joke, you know, I laugh about it. The same with my response. You make a joke about it because, God knows, if you're serious, that is a mistake. I think people drink and have sex and expect it to be great, but you're putting a burden on both of you and are bound to be disappointed.

"But people often associate wine, dinner, maybe some cognac, with going to bed, and then it's not as great as you thought it might be or should be or had been. It's amazing that people don't look to alcohol as the explanation.

"I'm not into drugs at all. I'm a person who likes to be in control. Sometimes you just feel like getting drunk, so you get drunk, but you're not looking to get laid. But then who the hell wants a hangover the next day? But you can titrate your dose of alcohol. The thing about taking cocaine or something like that is that once you take it, you have no control over it. No way would I ever do that.

"One of the problems about sex with the Brits, a hell of a lot of Brits, is that sex involves drinking. I am struck now when I go back to England as to how much drinking there is on social occasions. Not that I don't drink here, but much more there. And I think

150

that has an effect on how a lot of British women view sex, or respond to sexual intercourse."

## YOU HAVE TO LISTEN TO LEARN

George attributes much of his sexual awareness to the fact that he asks women about it, they tell him, and he listens.

"One of the problems between the sexes, and this is true in Britain as well as here, is that men do not listen. As I say, I like women so I like talking to them, and I talk *with* them, whereas most guys talk *to* women, they don't listen. A man tells a woman everything about himself; what does he know about her? Nothing.

"I'm just the reverse and I think that's what women have liked about me. I would let them do most of the talking. But men are so stupid because, usually, they go on about what they do and the woman has to sit there and tell him how wonderful he is. His favorite topic is himself."

## THE SEXINESS OF TALKING

Two-way communication and paying attention, George feels, are the keys to knowing what women want.

"Men in all generations don't understand the psychology of women. For one thing, they don't recognize the fact that her responses vary with her cycle. But if you're with a woman constantly, you know what her cycle is, or you should, and how her response differs. Some women, just before their period, don't want to be touched, whereas others are horny as hell. It's a very individual thing. So you have to be attuned to that, to her responses.

"Also, talking and warmth and talking after sex, just being close, is extraordinarily important, I've found. To talk to them before you go to bed, to talk to them when you're in bed, and to talk when you get up. It has a profound emotional response in a woman when a guy does that. Most guys don't, I'm afraid.

"I've only gathered this from talking to a lot of women. I only talk about my sex life with one male friend whom I've known for many years, and we're very up-front with each other. But with most guys, you don't because a lot of what men tell each other is bullshit, or else it's an embellishment of reality. You judge that by what the woman says. If a guy says, 'I did this, this, and this,' knowing them, I view that with a great barrel of salt, until I actually meet the woman."

## BEING YOUR OWN AUTHORITY

All this talking and observing has given George confidence in his conclusions. "I haven't seen the film, 'When Harry Met Sally,' showing how a woman can fake an orgasm, but there's no way a woman could

152

fake one with me. Because there are certain physiological responses of a woman, if you know them. You
can see how they could fake it easily if you're not attuned. Their pelvic muscles and their abdomen absolutely contract. Also, tension in the legs, and things
like that, if you're conscious of them, you know if they
have or haven't. There's flushing or the nipples become flaming red. Just for a very brief period. If you
know that, you don't have to ask."

George is a person who gives more credence to his
personal experience than to what society or science
says is supposed to happen:

GEORGE: I've been with women who have peaked
without having an orgasm. Well, I read an article
which said that the same thing can happen with
men. And I said, 'Christ, I knew it!' I knew I wasn't
a freak. I can have an erection and I'm almost
there but it—ejaculation—doesn't happen. And so
what? It still feels great. You do not have to judge
an orgasm by ejaculation. This article said you
don't have to ejaculate, or you can have multiple
orgasms, which has always been my case.

ME: What does that mean exactly?

GEORGE: I can make love and have an ejaculation
and still maintain an erection and stay in the vagina and have another ejaculation a minute or
two later, or maybe in twenty minutes, or not
ejaculate.

This myth that men peak at 18 and women don't
until later is total rubbish. The study has been

shown to be flawed. I'm a living example of it, for one thing. And I never believed it anyhow.

## CONSTANT LEARNING

And George, perhaps unlike other men of his generation, is able to base his conclusions on a fairly wide range of experiences:

"It's a constant learning process. I think every woman is different, there are no two women I've been to bed with who are the same, in their responses, just all the things they do. You cannot say women and sex and draw a detailed outline of this equals that, it's not possible. Every woman is different—that's my experience—in their sensitivity, in what they like and don't like, or like more. There's just a whole spectrum.

"You have to learn what gives them the most pleasure, it may please another woman but not her. So to say, 'Here's a sex manual and this is what you do' is totally misleading. A lot of guys really get led up the garden path, women as well, but more so men, i.e., in the sense that the man is supposed to take the lead, and that sort of jazz. But women's responsiveness is very different, from stimulation, direct stimulation, to caressing, very different. No two women are the same."

When I asked George how broad his sample population was he said: "I wondered if you would ask that and I wondered how I would answer it. Say two dozen. What the hell. That's a nice round figure. It's probably more than that but I, honest to God, have never kept a count, so I don't know. That's across my whole life. Certainly at least a dozen here in America. And of different ages, a generation apart."

## MERGERS AND ACQUISITIONS

The story of how George and his current girlfriend got together demonstrates George's dedication and resourcefulness when it comes to sex.

"Kate hadn't slept with a man for six years when we met at a party. I flew over on a Friday, met her on Tuesday, we went to dinner on Wednesday and got on very well. Then she went out to her cottage for Christmas. And just as she was getting into a cab after dinner, she said, 'Well, you can call me [at the cottage],' and she gave me the number. So then I call her, and it transpires that her daughters are only going to be there for a few days after Christmas. I said, 'Christ, if you're going to be on your own, I'll come down and see you.' She said, 'Oh, would you?' and I said, 'Yeah, I'll be down like a shot.'

"She met me next to the station, and we went back to her cottage, and after about ten minutes, we decided that we better go to bed or otherwise this is going to be a blown-out day. You know, it's going to be a wipe-out for both of us because we're so uhm—she hadn't been to bed with a man for six years. So we go to bed, and it's great, except—and this is a difference with age, although I've been this way when I was

155

younger too—she couldn't have an orgasm. She was almost there and it wouldn't happen. We tried every way, oral sex—well, I found it funny. But she was starting to get terribly distraught and worried, 'What's wrong with me? My God, what's happened to me?' I said, 'Jesus, don't worry about it. I've got an instant solution.'

"So the next day we went to buy a vibrator, okay? We go down in the part of town where you think there would be sex shops, but we didn't see them, so I wondered, 'How the hell am I going to find out where to buy one?' And then I saw a cab driver. I asked him and he told me, a couple of blocks away. The whole thing was as funny as hell.

"So we took it back, and my God—well, she had one and it's been terrific ever since. It's never been a problem, at all, whatsoever.

"This was fourteen months ago. So then I stayed with her for five days, and honest to God, we had the dog and we took him out for a walk every day, but exactly what we did on each day besides stay in bed or make love in the lounge or on the floor or upstairs, I don't know. I can't even remember what the hell we ate, but we must have eaten. It was fantastic, incredible.

"Then she came over here last April for three weeks. I said we're going to get in the Guinness Book of World Records for having sex twenty-two days straight. When she got back she said, 'Christ, no wonder I was exhausted.' "

## IT'S 10 P.M. DO YOU KNOW WHERE
## YOUR PARENTS ARE?

Once George and Kate decided that they wanted to spend the rest of their lives together, it was time to tell their respective kids. George and Kate were particularly nervous because they weren't necessarily going to get married.

"I was especially worried about my daughters' reaction, because it's a fact that children do not want to know about their parents' sex life. But my kids aren't stupid, although they think we are. Anyway, they said, 'Father, you're old enough to make your own choices.' They don't care.

"Kate's children were more concerned about it. It's very difficult to think of another man in your mother's arms. On the other hand, their father was never close to them. But New Year's eve, after everyone went to bed, [Kate's daughter and I] talked and she told me things that I'm sure she never told her mother. I wouldn't tell her either.

"So we got over that one with the kids, but that worried me more than anything else."

## FREQUENCY IS RELATIVE

When I asked George how often he and Kate make love, his answer was far more telling than a numeric figure tabulated in surveys.

"Sometimes we can go to bed and just lie there with no intention of doing anything—we would be tired or whatever—and then those hormones would start bubbling away, you know? So I would define it as most of the time. Maybe after a couple of years we'd slow down, I don't know.

"But I think it is a different thing after being married for thirty years. Right now, it's totally romantic, totally sexual, totally emotional, totally intellectual as well. So it's like a new life, but you have now all the experiences that have accrued over the years in relationships with others. You start with all these pluses."

## ACCENTUATING THE POSITIVE

George's attitude toward aging itself is very sexy: "In my experience, age is in the head. Certainly there are physical manifestations of age, you know, you get gray hair, but you don't have to resign yourself to anything. Kate just made her hair blond, and I encouraged her. I think women should wear makeup and try to look attractive at any age. I'm planning on dying my

158

own hair before I go back to see my kids [for the holi-days]. I guess the beard will have to go."

## LOVE CONTINUES TO MAKE THE WORLD GO ROUND

Accentuating the positive, feeling self-reliant, being communicative and an astute listener, and following his heart have made George a very happy, sexually active older man. In conclusion he told me:

"Being in love is great. There's nothing like it, that's what life is all about. Neither of us has that much money and that doesn't bother me, it doesn't bother her. We'll probably wind up in Spain somewhere, which I'd like to do, it's quite cheap there and we could live well in a shack. Having someone is what makes the world go round."

# Part III

# THE PATH TO GOLDEN SEX

# CHAPTER NINE

# PRESERVING SEXUAL HEALTH

*Reexamine all you have been told,*
*at school at church or in any book,*
*dismiss whatever insults your own soul . . .*

—WALT WHITMAN (1819–1892)
*This Is What You Shall Do*

THIS CHAPTER will describe what one can do to ensure a healthy older body, mind, and sex drive. It will discuss the role of attitude, exercise, and nutrition, and the possibilities of therapy, plastic surgery, and synthetic hormones.

## GOLDEN HEALTH

As I discussed in Chapter Two, health problems and their treatments may interfere with sex but there's a lot you can do before you toss in the towel. And sex itself can be a key to good health, so it seems worth the effort to preserve or enhance your desire and your ability.

The greatest chance of happiness, health, and love comes with the awareness that you are the person most able to know what's best for you. The most important thing in health is a sense of control. Therefore, learning to listen to your body and learning for yourself what is right for you, not feeling dependent on someone else to tell you, is the key to longevity in general, and to the longevity and quality of your sex life.

## APPRECIATING THE PRESENT

The point of focusing on sex in later life is not to tell people that they should be doing it or how to do it, but to encourage readers to enjoy every moment of their lives and to embrace the challenges of longevity as well as those presented at any other stage in life. In *The Path of Least Resistance*, Robert Fritz recommends that we stop comparing the present with the past, and appreciate the present as a unique moment with its own "meaning, purpose, possibility and existence." He explains that for those with a creative orientation versus a "reactive-responsive" approach, "reality is not a threat but a welcome experience." The happiest, sexiest golden agers appear to be those who have accepted themselves and their age.

## THE ADVANTAGES OF ADVANCING AGE

Indeed, advancing age can have its advantages. Those most often cited by golden agers are: no more fear of pregnancy, no more interference from birth control or menstruation, more time to engage in sex, no children to interrupt, no more work-related worries, and a greater appreciation of life and one's partner. Those who retire to warm climates tend to report the added advantages of greater relaxation and physical activity in general, and needing less clothing. "Summers were always our most romantic time," explains a 68-year-old woman who recently moved with her husband from New Hampshire to Boca Raton, Florida. "Now it's summer all year long."

There are also sexual benefits of experience and of knowing oneself, the product of a long life. As the protagonist in Barbara Raskin's novel *Hot Flashes* puts it: "Male desire and approval are less important to me now. Ditto for the approval of family, friends, and academic colleagues. How I feel in the presence of a particular person has finally become more important than how that person feels about me." Feeling more self-assured may explain why older women are more likely to initiate sex, to communicate what they like and don't like, and to enjoy it.

165

## GREAT EXPECTATIONS GIVE WAY TO GREATER POSSIBILITIES

Another advantage of being older is that one no longer has as many needs to fill by one's lover, i.e., fathering children, financial support, social status, etc., and therefore has fewer expectations that can lead to disappointment. One can choose one's partner based purely on physical/spiritual/intellectual attraction. It may be that one becomes less of a perfectionist as one ages, too. That makes the burden of fulfillment lighter for one's mate, and true love may be more possible than ever before.

On the other hand, Lee Roberts in Chapter Seven felt that she became more selective and less in need of company. That's another possibility. There's less pressure to be mated, if that's your preference. She says that even if she found someone special to share her bed—and she hasn't given up hope—she would still want him to have his own home to go back to.

## SEXUAL DISCOURSE

It has been documented that simply discussing sex can do more to alleviate sexual problems—from inhibition to impotence—than considerably more ambitious psychotherapeutic, behavioral, and other educational methods. It's understandable that today's golden agers might have the hardest time opening up about sex. Besides the difficulty in finding someone who will listen sensitively, feeling uncomfortable about expressing their sexual feelings has long roots.

A 1949 sex manual, *Handbook for Husbands (And Wives): A Complete Guide for Sexual Adjustment in Marriage*, was considered quite racy in its day, but the parentheses in the title alone reflect the uneasiness with which couples communicated about and engaged in sex. Even interest in sex for a woman was questioned. The book's author, Porter Davis, points out: "A book that dares to mention a couple engaging in relations more intimate than a kiss stands a good chance of being banned in Boston."

Many of the women I interviewed told me that they may have had sex for 20 years before they began to enjoy it, if they ever did. Some of them left or lost their husbands before discovering their sexuality. And if these women were so dissatisfied sexually, how happy could their men have been?

For some, like Rebecca MacDonald in Chapter Four, it takes professional therapy to overcome the impairment of sexual enjoyment caused by early misinformation. In her case, a concerned new lover broke the ice for her and led her to a therapist. Many others, unfortunately, give up on sex rather than seek ways to improve it, often because talking about it seems too hard or futile.

Bob White of Chapter Six is a prime example. After

167

his open-heart surgery, he stopped having sex and he didn't want to discuss it, not with his wife, definitely not with his doctor. His wife, Sue, told me that she learned to accept life without sex and that they developed other aspects of their relationship. She also developed arthritic hips and diabetes. Then her husband got prostate cancer. Maybe there's no connection, but certainly withdrawing physically from the relationship was not a healthy solution.

Even George Gibbons, who was quite communicative about his sexual experiences, didn't consult with his wife when he chose to curtail sexual relations with her after her mastectomy. He said he didn't want her "to feel that she *had* to" have sex. But how did he know that she didn't want to? As a result of not discussing it with her, she may have concluded that *he* didn't want to. And so on.

Good sexual communication is important at any age, whether or not there are problems; it is the key to sexual satisfaction. Talking helps cure anxiety; it's the surest way to find out how your partner feels and to let your partner know how you feel. Working to improve your sexual communication will help you and your partner develop a deeper trust, a greater sense of intimacy, and a feeling of adventure about your relationship.

Communicating effectively about sex takes practice, however, so don't give up if it's difficult at first. Recognizing that there is much to be gained should help give you courage. Here are some tips:

1. Share this book with your mate.
2. Pick or plan a time when you won't be interrupted and don't have to rush off anywhere.
3. Don't expect the other person to know how you feel; explain as fully and honestly as you can.
4. Accept all feelings and the right for the verbal expression of these feelings. For example, it is just as appropriate to say, "I feel angry when . . ." as it is to say, "I feel terrific when . . ."
5. Expect changes, but not miracles. Sexual communication requires continued dialogue.
6. If it's a friend with whom you wish to discuss your feelings, keep in mind that he or she may be as curious and as nervous as you about comparing notes. Someone has to take the initiative; your friend will probably be glad it's you and welcome your honesty.

Some books are entirely devoted to the subject of sexual communication. For an autobiographical account of an older couple learning to communicate about sex, read *Love Talk: A Model of Erotic Communication,* by Natalie and Ralph Bacon. Lonnie Barbach's *For Each Other* offers communication exercises for couples to aid sexual intimacy.

## SEXUAL THERAPY

Although there is a lot you can do on your own, and by talking things through with a mate or friend, sometimes it's important to have a professional's help with sexual problems. You may simply want an objective listener to offer support and encouragement. If you have a specific complaint such as impotence, pain, or decreased desire, the first step is to rule out any physiological culprit, so check with your physician. Even if you head straight to a sexual therapist, he or she may start by sending you to a physician for a physical. After that there are several schools of thought, and it's up to you to choose a therapist you feel comfortable with and have confidence in.

William Masters and Virginia Johnson, for example, believe sexual problems are couple problems and therefore treat both partners, rather than just the person reporting the dysfunction. Generally, their model of therapy involves a daily two-week program conducted by a male-female therapy team, one of whom is a physician. They report an average cure rate for all sexual dysfunctions of 80 percent, with a five-year relapse rate of five percent. Sexual therapist Barry McCarthy holds that most sexual problems stem from a lack of knowledge, from communication problems, or from psychological disorders, making psychologists, social workers, marriage counselors, and ministers theoretically qualified to help.

170

Most sexual therapy involves meeting with the therapist, first together and then individually, and carrying out sexual "homework assignments" between weekly sessions with the therapist. Therapy is generally short-term, not lasting more than six months.

Finding a therapist trained in counseling older clients may be a challenge. Don't get discouraged. The supply will have to increase with demand. In the absence of other referrals, try the Sex Information and Education Council of the United States (SIECUS) at 122 East 42nd Street, New York, NY 10017, or the American Association of Sex Educators, Counselors and Therapists (AASECT), 11 Dupont Circle NW, Suite 220, Washington, DC 20036, for the name of someone in your area.

## TOUCHING WORDS

A lot of what sexual therapy consists of is called sensate therapy, focusing attention on non-genital touching. After an initial period of abstinence from intercourse, to reduce anxiety and facilitate communication, couples are encouraged to simply touch one another in exploratory ways, without the goal of orgasm. "The single most powerful sensual path to erotic arousal is touch," says Nora Harlow in her book *Lover to Lover: Secrets of Sex Therapy.* Yet, an all-too-common reaction when mechanical trouble strikes is to give up completely, to *stop* touching.

Even in the best of sexual relationships, couples

171

can lose the freshness and excitement of discovering each other's bodies, drifting into repetition of their established physical repertoire. When what worked well for a while stops working, lovers may think of changing partners instead of simply changing repertoires. Over time, particularly if you're with the same lover or if what you've been doing *never* worked well for you, there's even more need to find new ways of enjoying each other, and the answer is at your fingertips.

The emphasis on erection and orgasm as the indicators of sexual prowess can get in the way of good sex, at any age. Erection is a reaction to eroticism; it's the eroticism that deserves the attention. Women who responded to my questionnaire repeatedly stated their desire to be touched and caressed, to have their lovers know their bodies, a finding consistent with others' studies of younger women. For men, like Martin Shaw in Chapter Five, it may take getting older to appreciate the pleasures and importance of touch, or "handling" as he calls it.

Therapists suggest taking turns, giving your full attention to either giving or receiving pleasure, for 30 minutes each on separate days. The idea is to focus your full attention on your arms one day, your lover's arms the next day, then your head, your lover's head, your legs, your lover's legs. Once you have explored the whole body, experimenting with where and what touch feels good and what feels even better, you can move on to the genitals, still without the goal of orgasm and without intercourse. You can use oil, feathers, fur, whatever you can think of, to expand your repertoire of touching. Finally, on the ninth day or so, you can experience penetration, but still spend a full 30 minutes concentrating on what feels good for one partner, and then 30 minutes the next day discovering what the other partner's pleasures are. Touching takes time, but if it feels good, what's the hurry?

Touching may be therapeutic as well as erotic. Massage—first used as a medical tool by the ancient Chinese and Greeks—dilates the blood vessels, improving circulation and relieving congestion and tension throughout the body. And therapeutic touch, a modified version of "laying on of hands," is a growing area of scientific investigation, showing promise as an effective method of healing, from low-back pain to cancer. So there may be more to touch than its immediate pleasures, and even more reason to indulge. (See later section on Reflexology for news on another type of massage.)

## TIMING

*When* you have sex may be a key ingredient in making it pleasurable and, in some cases, possible. Although lovemaking is usually a nighttime activity through one's younger years, that may be more by default than by choice. Many older people report greater interest in sex after a good night's sleep or an afternoon nap. "Making love during the day is a luxury I never had during twenty-five years of working and kids," says a 69-year-old retired department store manager.

173

For him and other golden agers, daytime becomes the best time.

Pain and stiffness, an often cited deterrent to sexual or any other activity, may be better or worse at different times of day. For example, some people, especially those with rheumatoid arthritis, feel worse in the morning, whereas osteoarthritis sufferers feel their *best* in the morning. If you are taking pain or anti-inflammatory medications, ask your doctor about how to time your intake so the drug is most effective when you want to make love.

A final word about timing: take your time. The more time you allow yourself to enjoy making love, the less pressure you'll feel, and the more aroused you can become. This is true at any age, but with age you may have more time and more need to go slow. Women often complain of men heading for penetration too soon, before they've had a chance to savor foreplay and to become aroused enough for the vaginal lubricants to flow. Older women may need even more time, as dipping estrogen levels can cause vaginal dryness. Men, too, may take more time and attention to be ready for intercourse. In the golden years, men and women may just find that their timing is more compatible than when they were younger.

## DESIRE STRAITS

In *Love and Sex After 40*, Dr. Robert Butler, a maverick in the field of gerontology, and his wife Myrna

Lewis, a social worker, offer encouragement for those with physical dysfunctions, but say that "it is more difficult, but not impossible, to treat low or absent sexual desire or lack of pleasure in sex." In her book *Lover to Lover: Secrets of Sex Therapy*, Nora Harlow, who is married to a sex therapist, says that loss of desire in long-time lovers "is the most common of all sex problems and the easiest to correct." Dr. Anthony Pietropinto and Jacqueline Simenauer recently published an entire book devoted to the subject called *Not Tonight, Dear: How to Reawaken Your Sexual Desire*.

## PENILE IMPLANTS

If impotence is a problem and all else fails, high technology has come to the rescue with devices that can help restore erection capability and possibly self-esteem. Penile implants or prostheses are still experimental and controversial, however. Depending on whom you ask, between 30,000 and 150,000 penile prostheses have been implanted since 1975, with three-fourths of these in men over age 50.

Prostheses are not a magic potion and they require surgery for insertion. Although several different models are available, some more or less obtrusive, prostheses are mechanical devices which may need repair or replacement. They last a maximum of seven years and cost approximately $7,000. They do not increase sexual desire or sensation. If you could climax before the surgery, you should be able to do so afterwards.

175

On the positive side, they do not interfere with ejaculation or fertility.

Generally, implant surgery is only performed when the impotence is a chronic organic problem, usually caused by injury to the spinal cord or pelvic nerves, or by vascular problems and diabetes. Estimates of organically-based impotence range between one and ten percent of all cases, though prostheses manufacturers claim the percentage is much higher. Once the prosthesis is implanted, there is no more chance of naturally-occurring erections.

Members from a club of penile implant recipients recently appeared on the Phil Donahue talk show, cheering prostheses manufacturers. Still, these devices should be viewed as a last resort.

For more information you can write to the manufacturers: American Medical Systems, Dacomed, Mentor, and Surgiteck, all in Minneapolis. Keep in mind, though, that they are in business to sell their products. Before making any decisions, be sure to consult with a physician who is not connected with a prostheses manufacturer.


## SYNTHETIC HORMONES

Some women swear by it, others never got to judge the difference since they may have started taking synthetic estrogen after a hysterectomy in their thirties. Although synthetic estrogen and other hormone replacement therapy may help prevent or postpone some so-called age-related problems, such as hot flashes (which at worst are only temporary), vaginal dryness, and osteoporosis, several studies link the drugs to cancer. Luella Klein, former president of the American College of Obstetricians and Gynecologists, told me that she had big hopes for ERT (estrogen replacement therapy) but finds recent studies discouraging. It is not a miracle drug nor is it harmless.

If your main reason for taking synthetic estrogen is vaginal dryness, consider other remedies first. Applying an over-the-counter water-based lubricant, such as K-Y jelly, just before intercourse may be sufficient. According to the Johns Hopkins medical newsletter *Health After 50*, you should avoid petroleum-based products and never use estrogen cream unless prescribed by a physician. Antihistamines should also be avoided; formulated to dry out mucus membranes, they don't stop at the vaginal walls. Soaps, bubble baths, detergents, and personal hygiene sprays can irritate sensitive vaginal tissue and cause dryness, too.

Once again, physicians may be too enthusiastic about prescribing drugs, and the promise of a quick fix can be appealing. Synthetic estrogen's benefits are mostly of short-term value (possibly decreasing hot flashes), and its risks, a far longer list (including increased risk of gallstones, uterine and breast cancer, and blood clots), are both short- and long-term.

## MATING GAINS

Although Lee Roberts, Chapter Seven, says she's happy living alone, statistics suggest that the absence of a spouse or other family member who can provide informal support for health and maintenance requirements is the most critical factor in the institutionalization of an older person. Therefore, pairing up, having companionship, sexual or otherwise, may be the best prevention against the problems of aging. For the five percent who are institutionalized, there should be more opportunity for socializing and privacy, something nursing home administrators are starting to recognize.

Women tend to age alone because they married older men. Even if they married men their own age, women would be likely to outlive them by six years or so. Until we figure out how to keep men around longer, maybe women should start seeking younger mates. Why should that option be limited to men?

Finding a mate once you are older and alone can certainly be hard, perhaps the biggest obstacle to sex in the golden years, as discussed in Chapter Two. But not impossible. George Gibbons lamented that he couldn't meet single older women, only women in their thirties and forties. "They don't go out," he observed. As Sue White said, the thought of going out as a single older woman is scary, awkward. She feels sorry for her single woman friends who are the odd-men-out at social dinners. But staying home won't cure solitude.

If you're over 50 today, you probably didn't experience being single long before you married. Your closest contact with any singles scene may have been through your children. That's okay. You know how to start a conversation, you've lived a long life, you have something to say. Find somewhere to say it or somewhere to learn something new. Even if there are only young people in the class, they may have single parents your age. And even if they don't, young people can be interesting and fun to be with, too. Or go on a group tour—of your local city, a museum, or the Canadian Rockies. The key is to get out there, to be active, and to look like you're looking. Remember that any awkwardness is temporary.

You may feel like a maverick but you are not alone. Lee Roberts invited her niece to visit her in Rome and she stayed with her for ten years. They shared friends and experiences and became best friends. Eighty-two-year-old Helen Strauss has dates several times a week. She is a member of museums and the public library, and invites men, young and old, to accompany her to their events. She has such a great time that she turned down a marriage proposal because it would have meant leaving town and giving up her freedom. There are no age limits if you don't subscribe to them.

On the other hand, some women don't want the responsibility of a mate after years of being tied to one. That's your prerogative. You don't have to get married and you don't have to be a caregiver anymore. Even some married couples opt to live separately and to "date" each other. The point is to have company, to have sex if, when, and how you want to, and to celebrate your golden years.

## FRIENDS FOR LIFE

Company can come from friends, and often they outlive mates. Lee Roberts may live alone but she has lots of friends. Another woman I spoke with who is 67, upbeat, and attractive, told me "I get strength from my friends. We're all in the same boat and we help each other. It's a challenge. If someone else's physical problem doesn't stop them, you realize that you shouldn't make a big deal of your own problems."

In a *New York Times* interview before the opening of a retrospective of her work, centenarian painter Theresa Bernstein gave this explanation for her longevity and her wide circle of friends: "I don't judge people. I accept them as they are. Other people want to change their friends. You can't change anyone. You don't push people into your mold. If you do that, you're never going to have a lot of friends. The secret of my survival is, I have many people."

## CONFRONTING THE FEAR

In the Self-Portrait of Sue and Bob White, Bob says that "aging ain't for sissies" and both tell of their pact to help the other "take a trip" if one were to become so ill as to be a burden to the other. They are not the only ones with this idea. One day, April 24, 1990, to be exact, I opened the *Washington Post* to find two stories about suicide: one involved a husband and wife, both 82, who had been married for 60 years; the other was 86-year-old Bruno Bettelheim, renowned psychologist and concentration camp survivor.

All three were long-time members of the Hemlock Society, which espouses chosen death. Although Bettelheim's death came as a shock to friends and relatives, Justin and Betty Bowersock had openly discussed their plans for years. Their daughter was quoted as saying: "When the time came that the quality of their lives was no longer the same and wasn't going to get better, they were going to—as Mother said —call it a day."

I was disturbed by these stories and the notion of ending one's life sooner than nature intended. As I thought about it, though, I realized that deciding when one's life will end is an extension of the idea that a sense of control over one's life is essential to health, vitality, and sexuality. The Hemlock Society's reasoning is that one need not fear death if one knows that it will happen by choice rather than by chance. And as

Lee Roberts laments in Chapter Four, the fear of becoming dependent on others can be even greater than the fear of dying. Perhaps planning to choose the time and circumstances of one's death could ease anxiety and result in greater quality of life. However, one still hates to see anyone toss in the towel before it's time.

## JOIE DE VIVRE

I prefer the notion of *carpe diem* to chosen death. It's not over, till it's over, and there's nothing sexier than a zest for life. You've probably gotten the message by now that I'm a big fan of NBC's sit-com "The Golden Girls," and I highly recommend that you tune in—if you aren't already—to see senior *bon vivants* in action.

In a particularly poignant episode, Dorothy (Beatrice Arthur), one of the main characters, has seen numerous physicians in search of an explanation for her assorted symptoms, such as swollen glands and tiredness, until she finds one who diagnoses her as having Chronic Fatigue Syndrome, a newly recognized illness. In celebration of finally knowing what's wrong with her, she and her three housemates go out to dinner at a fancy restaurant. Just as they are making a champagne toast, Dorothy spots one of the neurologists who examined her at another table and she can't resist giving him a piece of her mind. The dialogue goes something like this:

DOROTHY: Excuse me, Dr. Budd, you told me that I wasn't sick, that I was just getting old, and to see a psychiatrist. But it turns out that I *am* sick and my illness has a name. It's Chronic Fatigue Syndrome.

DR. BUDD: I'm sorry, but I don't remember you.

DOROTHY: Oh? Maybe *you're* just getting old. Dr. Budd, I came to you sick and you dismissed me. You made me feel like a fool, like a child. I suppose if I'd been a man, I would have been taken a bit more seriously, instead of being told to see a hairdresser.

DR. BUDD: Madame, if you don't mind, I'd like to enjoy my dinner in peace.

DR. BUDD'S DINNER DATE: (Her sympathies suddenly shifting to Dorothy) No, let her finish.

DOROTHY: Believe it or not, someday you're going to be on the other side, and as angry as I am, I still wish you a better doctor than you were to me.

The point is, if you don't get the information or the encouragement or the appreciation that you would like, keep looking.

As another Latin saying goes, *mens sana in corpore sano* (a healthy mind in a healthy body), and keeping mentally active is a key to retaining good health. That women have more freedom today to pursue a variety of careers may help keep them in good shape mentally, physically, and sexually. For men and women, retirement need not mark the end of one's productivity.

183

No matter what you have been doing—or not doing—until now, it's never too late to pursue something new. Here's some encouraging proof: "After raising two children, I took my civil service exam and started a new career at the age of 60," says a 63-year-old art reference librarian. "I feel better and have more energy now than when I was 40."

Studies have repeatedly shown that in a wide variety of fields, people are at their most productive and creative in early adulthood and then undergo a steady decline, but you don't have to buy that. For a story headlined "Why, in Some Fields, Do Early Achievers Seem to Be the Only Kind?", the *Washington Post* created graphs which showed a surprising pattern. While the line representing creative power rises sharply in the twenties and then declines, as predicted, it surges again after age 70 in fields such as physics and poetry.

University of California (at Davis) psychologist Dean Keith Simonton suggests that getting and developing ideas is not a biological function of age, but rather the typical consequence of being faced with a new intellectual environment. As a result, an aging society need not be unproductive if people enter new fields after their productivity peaks in a previous field.

He also concludes that when you peak depends on how many ideas you have. The legendary 19th-century mathematician K.F. Gauss, for example, is said to have begun his career with so many ideas that even a lifetime of feverish activity was not enough to explore them all. It's never too late to be creative, and even if you've run out of ideas in one area, trying something new may get your mental juices flowing again. As anthropologist Margaret Mead said, "The most creative force in the world is a menopausal woman with zest."

## GETTING PHYSICAL

Pain is probably the most common complaint among older people and the biggest deterrent to sex; ironically, sex, or other physical exercise, may be the best medicine. As noted in Chapter Two, physical activity —especially, but not only, sex—stimulates the body's release of endorphins, the body's own painkiller as well as mood elevator. As people get older they tend to be less physically active, walking instead of running, driving instead of riding a bicycle, sitting at a desk instead of playing outside with friends. As sedentarism sets in, endorphin production decreases, and stiffness, pain, maybe even crankiness increase. To stay pain-free, sexy, and happy, you need to keep active.

In addition to sex itself, any one of the following exercises will help gild the path to golden sex. All of them are gentle, so you probably won't have any trouble even if you've been inactive for a long time. However, it's a good idea to check with your physician before doing anything your body might find strenuous.

185

## KEGEL EXERCISES

In the 1950s, UCLA surgeon Arnold Kegel devised a series of exercises he hoped would put him out of business. He specialized in repairing flabby vaginal muscles, prolapsed bladders, and prolapsed uteri—in other words, organ changes caused by poor tone of the pubococcygeal (PC) muscles between the vagina and the anus. This area, known as the "pelvic floor," slackens during pregnancy and childbirth. But good muscle tone can be restored and maintained, Kegel found, through faithful practice of simple exercises.

Kegel devotees claim the exercises improve sexual functioning, promote perineal muscle tone, relieve hemorrhoids, correct stress incontinence, and prevent prolapse of the uterus.

To perform a Kegel exercise, tighten the muscles of the pelvic floor, hold for a count of five, and then slowly release. A good way to find which muscles to tighten is to try to stop the flow of urine while urinating. For maximum effect, they should be repeated 50 to 100 times a day. Kegels can be done anywhere, at any time, while sitting, standing, eating, driving, even making love.

## SWIMMING

As Martin Shaw in Chapter Five observed, swimming improves muscle tone and increases endurance. In his case, he had bladder problems that ceased after he started swimming. I can't find any data to support a connection but I have heard many other anecdotal reports of swimming's healing ways. Buoyancy makes it a natural for osteoporosis and arthritis sufferers. And you don't have to swim to enjoy the benefits of being underwater; many pools offer aquatic aerobics and other exercise programs for older adults.

## WALKING

Going for walks can be relaxing, refreshing, social, and educational as well as physically beneficial. You can take a tour of a new neighborhood or simply stroll around the block. If you live near a beach, walking barefoot on sand can be particularly fun; the sand massages your feet as you walk and acts like a pumice to smooth the soles of your feet. Walking on sand also works your calf muscles slightly harder than walking on flat ground. While you are at it—or even if you are not up to sand-walking—you can collect seashells, listen to the waves, and inhale the ocean breeze.

There now are walking clubs that organize walks for members in shopping malls and other controlled environments so that you don't have to worry about dogs, traffic, getting mugged, or the elements.

## DANCING

Dancing is fun, it's social, and it's a great form of exercise. Recently, I took a ballroom dancing course in the adult education program at Stuyvesant High School in Manhattan. Many of my classmates were regulars

187

from the nearby Stuyvesant housing complex, largely populated by senior citizens. My 75-year-old partners could samba longer—not to mention better—than the young men in the class. Several of the older members of my class told me that dancing was their main source of exercise, and they were good advertisements for it. Many community centers offer ballroom dancing courses, either for free or a moderate fee.

When the Arthur Murray Dance Studio turned 75, the *New York Daily News* ran a story profiling an older couple who met, courted, and then married, thanks to Arthur Murray. Ida Kuna, a former secretary at a Westchester High School told the *Daily News:* "We'd each lost our spouses, and as far as I was concerned, there was no room in my life for the singles scene. I always loved to dance, though, and I found this was a very comfortable place for me to come by myself. Everyone's here because they like to dance. It's not like a singles bar. No one's standing around checking you out." Husband Emanuel added that they'll continue dancing "as long as we can lace up our shoes." Arthur Murray himself lived to age 95.

Judy Schwartz, an associate professor of dance education at New York University, believes that all older people can benefit from dance, regardless of whether they're healthy or suffer from arthritis, Alzheimer's disease, depression, or other afflictions. A golden ager herself, she conducts dance workshops at senior centers, nursing homes, and hospitals. She tries to give her older students "a creative, social, and body experience" by encouraging them to "think, imagine, remember, and interact." Whether it's a square dance or improvisational movements, participants can build strength, coordination, and flexibility, she says. Sometimes she has them stretch in a circle, imagining that they are pushing away anything they would like, such as loneliness, sickness, and pain. Then she asks them to pull out whatever they want: good health, close friends, pleasant memories, etc. "Creative dance lets older people choose how they want to express themselves," she points out, and feeling in control is healthy in itself.

## YOGA

I can't advocate yoga enough. Shelly Greenberg, former president of the Mid-Atlantic Yoga Association, says that yoga can help improve your physical and mental condition, no matter what kind of shape you're in when you start. "The breath is the focus of yoga. If you can breathe, you can begin." Gentle movements coupled with an emphasis on breathing work to tone the body inside and out. Yoga doesn't stress your body the way other physical activities can. In fact, it can be used as physical therapy for specific ailments or when other forms of exercise are too difficult. You can do it at your own speed and it can be practiced anywhere, without special equipment or clothing. If you have privacy, I highly recommend doing it in the buff so that you can see all of your body, especially your rib cage, as you breathe and stretch. Incorporating meditation practices, yoga teaches the art of balancing body, mind, and spirit.

These are my exercise favorites. If you're playing tennis four times a week like 69-year-old Bob White, you don't need me to tell you the benefits of being physically fit. Any activity that you enjoy, to whatever extent that suits you, will increase your energy and fitness level. You'll reap the rewards in bed and out (as long as you don't overdo it).

## DIET

There is no question that what you eat affects your mood and your health, and your mood and health affect how sexy you feel. The role of nutrition in disease is just starting to be appreciated, and the elderly, especially those who live alone, are likely to be malnourished. Poor diet can produce lethargy, disorientation, and dizziness—symptoms that can be misinterpreted as those of illness and treated with drugs instead of nutrients. And if there is something wrong physically, malnutrition can make things worse.

Zinc deficiency has sometimes been implicated in sexual dysfunction because it may interfere with hormone production. Zinc is present in most foods, so it's hard not to get the recommended daily allowance of 15 milligrams, but shellfish, seafood, meats, and certain whole grains, nuts, and green beans are particularly rich in zinc. Most multiple vitamins also contain zinc.

Several studies suggest that eating less may help you live longer and healthier. Mice who consume half the calories but 100 percent of the vitamins, minerals, and protein they need live 50 months and beyond, compared with the average mouse life span of 36 months. Even more impressive, researchers report that the calorie-conscious mice have better immune systems, stronger hearts, kidneys, and livers; more youthful levels of important hormones; fewer cataracts; and more pliant skin. They are also more alert, active, and higher-scoring on maze-learning tasks. Although scientists aren't sure why, some propose that the test animals metabolize their food more efficiently, thereby wearing out their bodies at a slower rate and staying younger. Whether what's true for mice applies to man remains to be proven, but certainly keeping light, as long as you get the necessary nutrients, will help you feel fit.

On the other hand, for women who find they have gained weight since they were younger, that may be healthy, as long as it's not more than ten pounds. The body stores estrogen in fat, so the female body needs a little padding for hormonal protection.

There are many different theories about what you should eat. The main thing is to make sure that you are eating well, and it may help to eat as many meals with friends as possible.

*Delicious Sex*, written by *New York Magazine*'s food critic Gael Greene, gets five stars for wit and inspiring suggestions. From how to eat a fig to stocking a bed-side refrigerator, she provides "a gourmet guide to pleasure for women and the men who want to love them better."

## APHRODISIACS

Through the ages various foods have been thought to be aphrodisiacs. Oysters are one of them. Legend has it that Casanova ate 50 every night before setting out to slay the ladies. Napoleon ate generous helpings of oysters on the eve of his conquests, which may say something about the military impulse. Today, oyster bars abound. Can science support the sexiness of oysters?

According to the Center for Science in the Public Interest, oysters are packed with nutrients. A half cup of raw oysters provides 750 percent of the recommended daily allowance of zinc, 12 percent of vitamin B2, eight percent of B1, five percent of calcium, and 46 percent of iron. One would have to eat six cups of wheat germ to get that much zinc and 35 large prunes to get that much iron, not a very sexy thought. But so far these scientists are saying only that oysters are healthy.

According to Greek mythology, Aphrodite, the Greek goddess of love for whom aphrodisiacs are named, sprung from the sea, so that may explain the marine origin of so many other alleged aphrodisiacs. Take caviar, hailed since the time of Homer. Then there's lobster and clams. Some experts speculate that seafood appears to have aphrodisiac properties because it is rich in phosphorus, a bladder excitant. Others note that the physical structure—particularly of clams and oysters—suggest the female sex organ.

The structure of peaches, with their fuzzy clefts, also seems to have made them a popular aphrodisiac in 18th- and 19th-century Europe. A "peach house" became English slang for a brothel, and a sexually alluring woman was (and still is) called a "peach" in virtually every European language.

The male sex organ is also represented among an array of aphrodisiacs, including the rhinoceros horn (powdered for consumption), the pickle, the mushroom, and the mandrake root (an ingredient in many recipes for the famous, and potentially deadly love potion, Spanish Fly).

There's more convincing evidence for the lures of chocolate and honey. Their high carbohydrate content dramatically raises the brain's production of serotonin, a neurotransmitter that generates warm, mellow feelings. Recent, highly sophisticated studies of chocolate have shown small amounts of phenylethylamine, another brain chemical, which many researchers believe is produced in response to erotic attraction.

Proving the effectiveness of any aphrodisiac is tricky and usually not a high scientific priority. If something works for you, that's evidence enough. Enjoy!

## VITAMINS

The same goes for vitamins. For some reason science is shy of endorsing vitamins, and it may be that what comes in a bottle may not work as well as what you can get from their source. But if you use moderation as your guide, most bottled vitamins can't hurt and may help. Vitamin C boosts immunity and vitamin E increases energy and cell repair.

## REFLEXOLOGY

Reflexology is an Oriental foot massage technique based on the belief that if your feet feel good, your whole body feels good. A foot massage can knead out the pressure in your body and your mind, and it's a wonderful, intimacy-building treat. One advocate told me that she and her mate use foot massage when neither is feeling particularly sexual. "It's like discovering a new erogenous zone," she says.

According to Lydia Sarfati, esthetics director of the Repechage Treatment Center in New York, the best way for a couple to use reflexology is to take turns massaging each other's feet—giving it your full concentration ideally for a half hour or more. She suggests using aromatherapy oils—lavender, musk, and patchouli are especially sensual.

Some basics: The person being massaged lies down;

the giver sits. Use one hand to support the foot and the other to massage. You can press with your thumb, rub in circular motions with your fingers, or knead softly with your knuckles—whatever feels good. A foot massage should not be painful. Start with the toes and work down to the heel. Don't forget the back of the heel—massaging it is supposed to be sexually stimulating. To learn more about reflexology, check with adult education centers, massage centers, and health clubs in your area to find day or weekend seminars.

## ART

Did you love to draw until second grade, when your teacher said your trees looked like bushes? Many people are discouraged while young and stop drawing and expressing themselves forever. But in expressing your creativity, art can be a path to increasing your sensitivity. Proof that it's never too late: Anna Mary Robertson ("Grandma") Moses began painting when she was in her seventies and lived to be 101.

In the same way that the fitness movement said that anyone, not just varsity athletes, could benefit from and enjoy sports, people at the Topnotch Spa in Stowe, Vermont, believe that everyone, not just artists, can enjoy the creative arts. A professionally equipped art studio is part of the spa because "it's an extension of our philosophy of wellness," says president John Lopis.

"Our goal is to get people beyond evaluating what they do, to enjoy doing it," says Lisa Beach, art director at Topnotch. "People don't worry about how they talk," she points out. "Art is just another form of communication." Beach helps participants get beyond their inhibitions by exposing them to a variety of materials—charcoals, pastels, bamboo pens and ink, oil crayons, watercolors. "People always say, 'I can't even draw a straight line.' Well, maybe you draw beautiful sensuous curves," says Beach.

## GOLDEN HONEYMOONS

One of the privileges of seniority is discounted travel prices and packages. Retirees have the advantage of a relatively open calendar, making travel possible when prices are most attractive. And traveling—changing the scenery and discovering new places—can be exciting and sexy. One couple, in their early seventies, told me that every time they take a trip they pretend that it's their honeymoon. But not having a traveling companion shouldn't keep you from venturing out. Lee Roberts feels she found herself, as well as the love of her life, when she went abroad alone.

Travel information changes all the time, so check with your travel agent for the latest senior citizen specials. Or ask your smiling friends where they've just been.

196

## KEEPING BEAUTY

It's almost reached the point where not having cosmetic surgery is embarrassing. Lifting and tucking has become such a big business it would seem that everyone is doing it. Well, that's not what I found. Nearly all of the women who responded to my questionnaire said they had never had cosmetic surgery and they never would. It's an option.

But wanting to look your best is another story. A special makeup artist network for cancer patients was created on the premise that looking good makes you feel better, and the Center for Human Appearance at the University of Pennsylvania seconds the idea. An interdisciplinary team of 20 consulting specialists offers plastic surgery, dermatology, nutrition, cosmetology, dentistry, and psychiatry all under one roof. They believe that how you look affects how you *function.* The Center's psychiatrist, Michael Pertschuk, says, "If people are bothered by a physical feature, they may quite possibly be less effective in other areas of their lives." And that goes for sex.

But he and his colleague also recognize that attractiveness is more than meeting a particular esthetic standard, and stress that they are helping patients to make the most of what they have rather than making dramatic changes. James Leyden, the Center's dermatologist, points out that most of the things that we've come to associate with aging—wrinkles, age

197

spots, sagging skin—are due to past and present sun exposure. He recommends using sunscreen with at least a sun protection factor (SPF) of 15, at any age, even in winter, and predicts that doing so may "put plastic surgeons and dermatologists out of the aging-skin business."

As George Gibbons said, "You don't have to resign yourself to anything." He encouraged his girlfriend to color her hair and plans to dye his own and shave his gray beard. He believes in accentuating the positive. And approaching life in that way is probably the most important element in feeling and looking your best.

## IN CELEBRATION OF AGE

I find it encouraging that so many older people feel good about themselves just the way they are. Over the course of a long life, they have learned who they are and to accept themselves, to make the most of each day, and to embrace the continuous changes and challenges of life. The result can be very sexy. Maybe the rest of society could learn something from its older members.

*Three passions, simple but overwhelmingly strong, have governed my life: the longing for love, the search for knowledge, and unbearable pity for the suffering of mankind. These passions, like great winds, have blown me hither and thither, in a wayward course, over a deep ocean of anguish, reaching to the very verge of despair.*

*I have sought love, first, because it brings ecstasy—ecstasy so great that I would often have sacrificed all the rest of life for a few hours of this joy. I have sought it, next, because it relieves loneliness—that terrible loneliness in which one shivering consciousness looks over the rim of the world into the cold unfathomable lifeless abyss. I have sought it, finally, because in the union of love I have seen, in a mystic miniature, the prefiguring vision of the haven that saints and poets have imagined. This is what I sought, and though it might seem too good for human life, this is what—at last—I have found.*

*With equal passion I have sought knowledge. I have wished to understand the hearts of men. I have wished to know why the stars shine. And I have tried to apprehend the Pythagorean power by which number holds sway above the flux. A little of this, but not much, I have achieved.*

*Love and knowledge, so far as they were possible, led upward toward the heavens. But always pity brought me back to earth. Echoes of cries of pain reverberate in my heart. Children in famine, victims tortured by oppressors, helpless old people a hated burden to their sons, and the whole world of loneliness, poverty, and pain make a mockery of what human life should be. I long to alleviate the evil, but I cannot, and I too suffer.*

*This has been my life. I have found it worth living, and would gladly live it again if the chance were offered me.*

—Bertrand Russell (1872–1970)
*Autobiography*

CHAPTER TEN

# YOU HAVE THE LAST WORD

The April 25, 1990, Ann Landers column contained a
letter from a woman in her late fifties who wonders
whether she and her husband are peculiar. Twelve
years ago they decided that "sex was not important to
us and agreed to take it off our agenda." She says that
she and her husband "consider our marriage one of
the best" but "there has been so much glamorization
and exploitation of sex these days that we would be
embarrassed if our friends became aware that it is not
a part of our lives."

I can't help feeling sorry for a couple who have their
health and each other and choose not to be physically
loving. Maybe they will change their minds when they
get older. Or maybe I will. In any case, this woman's
letter demonstrates the power of society's influence on
whether we have or give up having sex, and the need
for an opportunity to compare notes.

In this book, I have explored the possibilities of sex
in the golden years. Not having sex is always an option, and some people are happy with that. The point

is not to say that one must have sex, just as assuming that older people cannot have sex is wrong. The point is to share information, to know that there are always choices, and that no one has to necessarily give up on anything just because of age.

From the stories presented here we have learned that the biggest potential impediments to sex in the golden years—prescription drugs, alcohol, performance anxiety, communication deficiency (between couples and between patients and physicians)—can be eliminated if you put your mind to it. You may have to lose weight, quit smoking, start exercising, face your fears, and/or seek therapy, but these are healthy, self-affirming activities with high payoffs in and out of bed. If sex serves to motivate you, great! Logistical problems such as lack of a mate or privacy can also be overcome. Above all, you need not let the past negatively influence your present. If your sexual responsiveness is different than it used to be, don't just throw in the towel. Experiment with new ways of making love. If sex wasn't that great before, you may discover that it can be better than ever *now*. The aging process, it turns out, is not something to fear; it's a chance to continue experiencing life and love with the advantages of greater self-knowledge and an ever-increasing perspective. How sexy!

Of course, the experiences of today's older people may be different for the next generation. Those who are not yet old, the Baby Boom generation and younger, generally have had more opportunity to explore their options and experiment sexually before marriage than today's golden agers did. Baby Boom and younger women are more likely to achieve financial independence before and during marriage. Marrying later, not at all, or several times, is much more common now. And roles and expectations within relationships are, to some extent, more flexible. Such variables may very well affect the sexual and romantic experiences of tomorrow's old. But there is, no doubt, a lot to be gained from understanding the path of our elders.

I, for one, am happy to know that I can look forward to sex in the golden years. What nicer form of exercise and health maintenance than to make love, and how encouraging to know that romantic love is always possible. Maybe my generation won't have the benefit of being with the same mate for 50 years—as we tend to marry later and divorce more frequently—but we have the knowledge, thanks to golden agers speaking out, that what's ahead can be worth aging for.

APPENDIX

# THE QUESTIONNAIRE

This questionnaire, used in the early research for this book, was distributed to women nationwide. It may be helpful for both male and female readers to consider how they would have responded.

Dear Respondent:

This questionnaire has been designed to help assess how women feel about getting older, in general, and how getting older affects sexual feelings and sexual relations. There is very little research in this area. Female sexuality only recently has gained attention as more than simply the complement to male sexuality. But sexuality in older women remains largely undocumented.

By answering the questions below, you will be assisting an attempt to learn about the aging experience and ultimately to share the findings in a book. Your response will help ensure that the questionnaire's results are representative.

You may remain anonymous, so please answer the questions as honestly and openly as you can. When you have finished, please mail the questionnaire to the address above.

If you would be willing to be interviewed personally, please let us know how we may reach you.

Thank you for your time and effort.

The first twelve questions call for basic background information. Please circle your answer to each multiple choice question.

1. What is your age? _____

2. What is/was your occupation? _____

3. What is your annual income? _____

4. How would you describe your present employment situation?
   a) Full-time
   b) Part-time
   c) Temporarily unemployed, looking for work
   d) Not employed
   e) Retired
   f) Other _____

5. If retired, how do you spend your time now? ___
   _____

6. What is your educational background?
   a) Less than high school
   b) High school graduate
   c) Some college
   d) College graduate (Major: _____)
   e) Graduate school or more (Degree: _____)

7. What is your religion? _____

8. What is your present marital status?
   a) Married
   b) Widowed

c) Divorced
d) Separated
e) Single (never married)

9. If [ever] married:
How long have you been/were you married?
_____

Have you been married more than once?
Yes _____ No _____
What age(s) were you when you got married?
_____

10. Do you have any children? Yes _____ No _____
How many? _____
How old were you when you had your children?
_____

11. What kind of housing are you living in?
a) Own house
b) Child's house
c) An apartment
d) A senior citizen complex
e) A nursing home
f) Other _____

12. What is your zip code? _____

The following questions call for more thought and de-tail than the previous ones. If you need more space than is provided, please use separate sheets of paper. If you find that the questions are too restrictive or not appropriate enough to your situation, please feel free to tell your story as you wish. The important thing is that this project includes what you have to say.

207

13. How do you feel about your age? Do you feel "old"? How do you define "old"? _____
_____
_____

14. Do you feel differently about your age than you thought you would? How do your previous expectations compare with your current situation? _____
_____
_____

15. Do you feel satisfied with your life so far? Yes _____ No _____ Why or why not? _____
_____

16. Is there an age of your life that you would return to if you could? What age and why? _____
_____

17. How do you feel about your physical appearance?
_____
_____

18. Do you do anything special to look and feel fit, such as take vitamins, follow a specific diet, or exercise? _____
_____

19. Have you had cosmetic surgery?
a) Yes (When and what kind? _____ )
b) No (Would you consider having it? Yes _ No _)

20. How might you feel differently at your age if you were a man? What else might affect how you feel about your age? _____
_____

21. How do others, particularly (potential) sexual partners, perceive/treat you differently, if at all, than when you were younger? _____

_____

_____

22. What changes have you observed in men, or in your perceptions of them, over time? _____

_____

_____

Now it's time for the heart of the matter:

23. How often do you make love, if at all? _____
Would you prefer to make love more often or less often? _____

_____

24. Does making love include intercourse:
a) Always
b) Most of the time
c) Some of the time
d) Never

25. Do you have a regular partner or partners?
Yes ____ No ____ If so, are you satisfied with your partner(s)? Yes ____ No ____ If unsatisfied, why? _____

_____

26. Since age 50, have you ever had a sexual relationship with:
a) A younger man? Yes ____ No ____ (Age difference? _____)

b) Another woman? Yes ⎯⎯ No ⎯⎯

c) A man other than your husband (if married)?
Yes ⎯⎯ No ⎯⎯ If you have had any such relationships, please describe. ⎯⎯⎯⎯⎯⎯⎯⎯⎯⎯

⎯⎯⎯⎯⎯⎯⎯⎯⎯⎯⎯⎯⎯⎯⎯⎯⎯⎯⎯⎯⎯⎯⎯⎯⎯

27. What do you consider the most important qualities in a lover? Is this different from how you've
felt in the past? ⎯⎯⎯⎯⎯⎯⎯⎯⎯⎯⎯⎯⎯⎯⎯

⎯⎯⎯⎯⎯⎯⎯⎯⎯⎯⎯⎯⎯⎯⎯⎯⎯⎯⎯⎯⎯⎯⎯⎯⎯

⎯⎯⎯⎯⎯⎯⎯⎯⎯⎯⎯⎯⎯⎯⎯⎯⎯⎯⎯⎯⎯⎯⎯⎯⎯

⎯⎯⎯⎯⎯⎯⎯⎯⎯⎯⎯⎯⎯⎯⎯⎯⎯⎯⎯⎯⎯⎯⎯⎯⎯

28. Have you noticed changes in your sex drive over
the years? Yes ⎯⎯ No ⎯⎯ If yes, please
describe. ⎯⎯⎯⎯⎯⎯⎯⎯⎯⎯⎯⎯⎯⎯⎯⎯⎯⎯⎯⎯

⎯⎯⎯⎯⎯⎯⎯⎯⎯⎯⎯⎯⎯⎯⎯⎯⎯⎯⎯⎯⎯⎯⎯⎯⎯

29. Do you have orgasms? If so, how regularly? Do
you orgasm more or less easily than you used
to? ⎯⎯⎯⎯⎯⎯⎯⎯⎯⎯⎯⎯⎯⎯⎯⎯⎯⎯⎯⎯⎯⎯⎯

⎯⎯⎯⎯⎯⎯⎯⎯⎯⎯⎯⎯⎯⎯⎯⎯⎯⎯⎯⎯⎯⎯⎯⎯⎯

30. Do your orgasms feel differently than they used
to? How? ⎯⎯⎯⎯⎯⎯⎯⎯⎯⎯⎯⎯⎯⎯⎯⎯⎯⎯⎯

⎯⎯⎯⎯⎯⎯⎯⎯⎯⎯⎯⎯⎯⎯⎯⎯⎯⎯⎯⎯⎯⎯⎯⎯⎯

⎯⎯⎯⎯⎯⎯⎯⎯⎯⎯⎯⎯⎯⎯⎯⎯⎯⎯⎯⎯⎯⎯⎯⎯⎯

31. What forms of stimulation can bring you to orgasm? Intercourse alone? Intercourse with addi-
tional stimulation? Other stimulation with a
partner? Masturbation? How has this changed
over time, if at all? Please describe. ⎯⎯⎯⎯⎯

⎯⎯⎯⎯⎯⎯⎯⎯⎯⎯⎯⎯⎯⎯⎯⎯⎯⎯⎯⎯⎯⎯⎯⎯⎯

⎯⎯⎯⎯⎯⎯⎯⎯⎯⎯⎯⎯⎯⎯⎯⎯⎯⎯⎯⎯⎯⎯⎯⎯⎯

⎯⎯⎯⎯⎯⎯⎯⎯⎯⎯⎯⎯⎯⎯⎯⎯⎯⎯⎯⎯⎯⎯⎯⎯⎯

_____

_____

32. Do you masturbate? Yes ____ No ____ How
    often? _____
    Has this changed in any way from the past?
    Yes ____ No ____ If so, how? _____

_____

33. Do you have sexual fantasies? Yes ____ No ____
    If so, please describe one. _____

_____

Questions 35–44 relate to circumstances or health
problems that may affect sexual relations.

34. Do you have/ have you had any problems—un-
    related to health—that have interfered with your
    sex life?
    Yes ____ No ____ Please describe. _____

_____

35. If you have had any problems, have you been
    able to solve them? How? _____

36. How old were you when menstruation ended? __

37. How did/does menopause affect you, if at all?

_____

38. Have you had a hysterectomy? Yes ____
    No ____ If so, when? _____
    How has that affected you? _____

_____

39. Are you taking estrogen? Yes ____ No ____ If
    so, since when and why? What are its effects?

_____

40. What other medication(s) are you taking, if any?

_____

How does/do the medication(s) affect your sexuality, if at all? _____

_____

41. Do you have or have you had any health problems, such as:
    a) Cancer (Please specify _____)
    b) Osteoporosis
    c) Diabetes
    d) Hypertension
    e) Other(s) _____
    What are/were the effects on you sexually, if any? _____

_____

42. What about your partner(s)? Have their health problems or medication interfered with sexual relations?
    Yes _____ No _____ Please explain. _____

_____

43. Has alcohol or drug abuse affected your sex life?
    Yes _____ No _____ If yes, how? _____

_____


The final section of this questionaire deals with sharing sexual information and defining generational differences.


44. Do you think your sex life could be better?
    Yes _____ No _____ How? _____

212

45. Do you discuss your sex life with anyone?
Yes ____ No ____ Whom? _____

46. Do you think getting/being older is different for you than it was/is for your mother? Yes ____
No ____ If so, how is it different? _____
_____

47. In what ways might sex at your age be different for your daughter, if you have one, or younger women in general? _____
_____
_____

48. Is there anything you wish you had been told about getting/being older and sex? _____
_____
_____

49. What advice, if any, would you give younger women about sex and getting older? _____
_____
_____

50. What other question(s) do you think this questionnaire should have asked? Please add any information or comments you would like. _____
_____
_____
_____

# Index